INTO THE
BOARDROOM

INTO THE
BOARDROOM

How to Get
Your First
Seat on a
Corporate
Board

D.K. LIGHT • K.S. PUSHOR

BEAVER'S
POND
PRESS

ISBN 13: 978-1-59298-689-7

Library of Congress Catalog Number: 2015919656

Printed in the United States of America
First Printing: 2016

21   20   19   18   17   16   6   5   4   3   2   1

Beaver's Pond Press, Inc.
7108 Ohms Lane
Edina, MN 55439–2129
(952) 829-8818
www.BeaversPondPress.com

*This book is dedicated to
those who choose to serve.*

TABLE OF CONTENTS

ACKNOWLEDGEMENTS

This book was an act of generosity, mentoring, and connection.

CEOs, directors, and senior executives—some of the busiest people in America—gave generously of their time and experience to make this book possible. Our continual requests for interviews and quotes, background information, or reviews of early drafts were met with efficiency and graciousness. Although many of these individuals are named within the text or on the cover, countless others contributed to our research and we wish to express our appreciation.

Reaching out to the next generation of corporate directors, making their way into the boardroom less of a mystery, and helping to expand the circles of talent from which the next directors will be chosen was an act of mentoring. It would not have been possible without the early support, example, and encouragement of executives like Jim Kunkel, Jeff McKeever, and Larry Downes, who mentored us along the way.

Connections. Our friends, professional associates, business colleagues, co-workers and community contacts—these are the very backbone by which a book like this comes together. We did not begin this project with everything we needed. But, we knew where to start and who to ask. To each of you who responded, "How can I help?" you have our heartfelt thanks.

And, on a personal note to our husbands, Ernie and John, and to our many children and grandchildren who have graciously accepted the decades of board meetings and conference calls required by our commitment to board service, and the time needed to complete this second edition of "the book"—thanks for your patience.

Dorothy K. Light
Denver, Colorado
December 1, 2015

Kathleen S. Pushor
Scottsdale, Arizona
December 1, 2015

INTRODUCTION:
THE CORPORATE
BOARD TODAY

Help Wanted: Over 70,000 positions exist for bright, talented individuals with proven track record of success. Must have integrity, sound business judgment, demonstrated financial acumen and superior communication skills. Industry knowledge and established network of key contacts required. Ability to tackle both the difficult and the delicate a plus. Must work well under pressure.

Ever seen an advertisement like this, recruiting qualified candidates to serve in one of most important positions in American business today—as a director on a corporate board? No, and you never will. Why? Because directors do not apply for a seat at the boardroom table, they are invited. This is a long-standing corporate tradition and one that is not likely to change anytime soon. It is not a particularly efficient process, and one that will be increasingly strained by the need to identify and attract new talent with high standards and fresh perspectives into the boardroom. This book introduces senior executives in our corporations, entrepreneurs in our small and mid-size companies, members of our professions, and those who serve our communities or teach at our universities, to the concepts of corporate governance and the process by which new directors are selected. This book can encourage a new generation of leaders to serve and prepare them to participate fully as they take their first seat on a corporate board.

Why bother? Because what happens in the boardroom makes a difference. Healthy, prosperous, innovative corporations are the backbone of a vibrant American economy. Successful corporations are the result of a unique, three-way relationship between the shareholders (who provide the capital), the management (who provided the vision and the human resources), and the customers (who purchase the goods or services produced). Board members balance these interests. When this engine is running smoothly, the results are limited only by our imagination—we can create jobs, invent gadgets, feed the world, cure disease, make movies, or send a man to the moon. When this engine runs amok, the results can be devastating to entire communities as jobs are lost, retirement savings evaporate, and investor confidence is shaken to the core.

The pressure is building on today's boards to enhance the quality and caliber of their members, just as pressure is mounting on those members to do a better job. Recent tales of director incompetence and accounting irregularities, reported in the business press, have heightened public concern. Many of these directors appear to have been over-worked with simultaneous responsibilities, stressed from the pressure of doing too much in too little time, or simply too trusting of the senior management or CEOs who mislead them.

This inattention by boards of directors—and their unwillingness to challenge current CEOs and their practices—can result in write-downs, lay-offs, poor financial performance, reduced dividends, stock price declines, and, in come cases, the bankruptcy or complete collapse of a corporation. In response to these unfortunate outcomes, savvy corporations are re-evaluating their boards and reaching out for talented and vigorous new directors.

In the past, the act of board recruitment was a mysterious process of selecting from a limited pool of friends and colleagues, often resulting in homogeneous groups that differed little from the company's own management team. An executive that was considered to be "safe" by virtue of their performance on Company A's board often found themselves invited onto several other boards as a result. Popular directors, many of them also active CEOs of their own companies, found themselves trying to serve on four or five at a time. Today that process is changing. Many corporations have recognized that they are better served by bringing in fresh talent, with adequate time for the task, and a new perspective to the table. In short, it's time for some new blood.

The business community appears poised for this change. In the most recent annual surveys published by the largest search firms, twenty-five to forty percent of the respondents stated that they are seeking younger, less experienced directors. Fifty-eight percent of the respondents said that their board has a first-time director, and eighty-one percent of the respondents thought their first-time directors were prepared to participate effectively.

Are you a candidate for service on a corporate board today? In the future? We wrote this book to answer that question for you and to advance the concept of board service as a career goal among a broader and more diverse pool of talent than has been considered in the past. As part of our research, we interviewed current and former CEOs and directors whose experience represents more than 100 corporate governance structures. Those interviewed included veterans of Fortune 500 boards, small and mid-cap publicly traded companies, venture-backed start-ups and large privately held corporations across the United States. We learned what works well in the boardroom and what doesn't. They told us what makes an effective director, what qualities and skills are important in the boardroom and what a CEO really wants from the board and from the individual director. We also picked up some practical advice about what doesn't work and what pitfalls a new director should avoid.

Seasoned executives told us repeatedly that diversity, not only of sex and race, but also experience, profession, age, and business perspective is critical to a company's long-term strategies and success. If American business is to respond to an increasingly volatile global economy, then management needs the exposure to a diversity of thinking and perspectives that will enable them to explore all the alternative courses available. A strong board can make this happen.

We also drew on our own personal experiences. We have each served as executives in Fortune 500 corporations and been on the other side of the table, making presentations to formidable groups of directors. We have each served on the boards of publicly traded companies, and had the experience of being interviewed, selected, and doing our time as "the new kid on the block" joining a group of more experienced directors around the table. And, we have appeared as panelists and speakers on this topic, reaping the benefit of many insightful and pointed questions from our audiences. Those questions taught us what it is that potential candidates need to know, or find hard to understand, about the process of becoming a director.

Corporate America needs to take a long, hard look at the significance of effective corporate governance and the individuals in whom they have placed this important trust. The financial press appears ready to keep up the pressure, and the headlines, until they do. The result will be an ongoing need for talented, experienced individuals with the integrity and willingness to accept a seat at the table. Currently, more than 50,000 positions exist for the director's of companies traded on the NYSE, NASDAQ and AMEX exchanges. At least another 20,000 seats exist around the tables of America's largest privately held companies. Who occupies these seats? What do they do? How were they selected? Could one of them be you? Let's find out.

PART I
THE BOARDROOM:
IS THIS WHERE YOU
WANT TO BE?

Want to know how to get your first seat on a corporate board? This book will tell you how. But first, we need to establish in your mind what board members really do; why they do it; and where they have a central conflict inherent in their role. We'll do that in Part I with our chapters on risk and reward, responsibility and duty, and the perspective of the CEO. Still interested? Then we'll help you determine if you have what it takes— the skills and experience to contribute at the board level, and if now is the right time in your career to take on this new role. You'll have all that figured out by the end of Part II. Finally, for those of you who are still in the running, we'll get down to the business of matching your preparation with an opportunity in Part III. We'll explain what the board member selection process is; how to get your name on the short list; what to expect in an offer; and, finally, we'll provide advice on how to become part of the team, gracefully, when you take that first seat on a corporate board.

By the time you finish reading, we will have taken the mystery out of the boardroom for you. You'll understand what goes on in there, what it takes to be a good board member, and whether this is a career goal that makes sense for you. You'll be hearing it straight from the horse's mouth—in anecdotes, personal stories, and advice from the CEOs and directors of over one hundred companies in America.

Yes, the mystery will be gone. But, the mystique will remain. The allure of business in a place where the stakes are the highest, the players are the brightest, and the game is by invitation only—the allure of the boardroom.

1

RISKS AND REWARDS

> The rewards of service are many. To name three: you get a new perspective that is helpful in your own career, you make new contacts, and you get to work with high caliber people. What more could you want?
>
> Don Procknow, former President and CEO, Western Electric.
> Former board member: J .P. Morgan; Ingersoll-Rand;
> and three other boards

Risk and reward go hand and hand in business. They are ever-present and their relationship to each other is ever-changing. Nowhere is this more evident than in the boardrooms of corporate America.

What attracts you to the boardroom? Probably the same thing that has attracted thousands of directors before you—money, power, esteem, and the chance to share talents and experiences. For most of us, the high stakes arena of big business is the most exciting game in town. Just what are the rewards? They can be substantial—professionally, financially, and personally.

Of course, choosing to serve in this arena also means taking a hard look at the risks involved—professional, financial, and personal risks.

Solving this equation of reward and risk is an individual matter. You must weigh these factors for yourself and arrive at your own conclusions. In this first chapter we will give you a closer look at the rewards involved, identify the risks our research has revealed, and let you listen in as seasoned directors answer our question, "Why do *you* serve on a corporate board?"

Then, you'll have to make up your own mind.

REWARDS

> Why? We serve on boards because of sharing, giving—and having that chance for wealth.
>
> Richard W. Perkins, CEO of Perkins Capital Management

The results of our research on the reward side of the boardroom equation surprised us. Of course, we expected to hear directors talk about making great connections or cashing in their options for a bundle. And in some cases substantial financial rewards did occur. But after all those interviews, the widespread conclusion that emerged was this: the most apparent reward for board service is professional, the most over-rated is financial, and the most lasting reward was personal.

PROFESSIONAL REWARDS

What is meant by professional rewards? We think it can be summed up as the change that occurs in your reputation. When describing the result of a financially rewarding opportunity, one can use dollars to assign a value. The results of a professionally rewarding experience are harder to quantify. We like to think of the professional growth that can result from board service as being denominated by the currency of your reputation—the sum total of your image in the marketplace. The experiences you've had, the transactions you've seen, the skills you've honed, the connections you've developed, the conversations you have been privy to, and the decisions you have made—these cause your reputation to grow in value or to be tarnished or diminished.

> All I have, ultimately, is my reputation.
>
> Kristine Garrett, former CEO, Bank One—Arizona

Joining a board can be very good for your reputation. Assuming the company has a strong image, is run by a bright and committed management team, and produces a socially redeeming product or service, it can be a very good association.

There is a certain cachet—a subtle message of making it—for executives who serve on an outside board. Regardless of the size of the company, just getting on a board that pays you for your input is an impressive credential. It tells the world that you are now on the other side of the table—that you have attained a significant milestone in the world of business.

Professionally, you benefit by expanding the context in which you can resolve business issues. Within your own company, you are focused on a narrow niche. Even if you are currently the CEO, you are only the CEO of one business. From your new vantage point on the board of another organization you can see things more clearly, less parochially.

> Directors have the opportunity to make contributions through the dynamic process of guiding an organization. They can move the perspectives away from narrow parochial views to a broader consensus of what is best for a company, and for all stakeholders concerned.
>
> Vincent J. Trosino, former President, Vice Chairman and COO,
> State Farm Mutual

If your current role is as president of a group of pharmacy retailers, you are deeply enmeshed in same-store sales comparisons, retail traffic patterns, digital couponing, and shopping center leasing negotiations. On the board of a bio-tech company that is involved in bringing research to the point where it can be patented and sold to a pharmaceutical company, produced and distributed as a new product—the world looks quite different. Now you see the bigger picture of the pharmaceutical supply chain: how legislation and regulations affect and sometimes stymie the testing and approval cycles, recruiting for talent, partnering with research universities and hospitals, gaining a patent, seeking distribution, and much, much more. The small, but important, role that your business has always played now comes into sharper focus. You see its role as one of the final links in a supply chain that may have begun decades ago in a research lab, and now finds completion over the pharmacy counter at your store in Des Moines.

Then the wheels start churning. Every director we spoke with came away from their experience with ideas and a fresh perspective. They got at least as much as they gave. One summed it up beautifully as, "Board service is the only way I have found to keep on getting my MBA, over and over, even though I graduated years ago. I never get tired of learning."

To have the opportunity to interact at this level of thinking with others is a privilege and a rare learning experience.

FINANCIAL REWARDS

A little extra money in your pocket or a new stock in your investment portfolio is almost always a good thing. The financial rewards of board service range from non-existent to modest to significant. Because of the broad disparities in personal financial gain realized, (as opposed to promised or those that remain perennially 'potential upsides'), we suggest that you view the financial aspect of board service as frosting on the cake. Certainly, seek to maximize it in every way, but if financial gain is your sole criteria for choosing to serve on a board, you would be better off making a direct financial investment in the company and not taking on the additional burdens and restrictions of a director.

Most directors are rewarded by a combination of cash and stock. Cash remuneration usually consists of an annual retainer, a per-meeting fee, and expenses. Stock rewards are usually a combination of an initial grant (of stock or of options) for coming onto the board, and then an annual grant of additional options or shares for each year of continued service. Companies with good governance practices encourage their directors to maximize their stock holdings. These grants either pay off because of appreciation over time or as the result of an event, such as the merger or acquisition of the corporation.

One significant indicator of how much financial reward you can get from board service is the size of the company you join. While some small companies are very generous, and some small companies (e.g., once upon a time Dell Computer Corporation was a very small company) do make it to the big time, rewarding their founding directors extremely well in the process, that is the exception, not the rule. In general, big companies have lucrative board packages, and small companies have modest plans. And some companies expect you to serve only for stock options.

Board members serving on the top Fortune 1000 companies do very well. Spencer Stuart, an international executive search firm, conducts an annual board survey of five hundred S&P companies. They reported that in 2014 the average annual retainer for S&P 500 directors was $107,383 compared to $49,727 in 2004. The highest board retainer was $300,000 paid by Prudential Financial and the lowest was $24,000 paid by People's United Financial. In addition to an annual retainer, some boards pay meeting fees, committee chair fees and committee member fees. These fees range from $1000 to $30,000. In addition, over 75% of the S&P 500 companies provide stock grants, up from 50% in 2004.

Ideally, the guidance provided by the directors in the board room translates into an increase in the value of the stock held by the shareholders. This benefit is then shared by the directors through the appreciation of their annual stock grants (outright granting of stock shares), RSU's (restricted stock units), or stock options.

Questions often surface about what happens to a director when a company is sold. Will you make a killing? Possibly. It depends on the company's performance. The best director compensation plans closely align the director compensation to the interests of the shareholders. If the shareholders win during the sale process, the directors also win. Many companies put in place parachutes and other legal provisions that protect not only the senior officers, but the directors as well. Called anti-takeover provisions, the goal is to protect the officers and directors from a sudden loss of employment and income. Generally, they contain a clause that fully vests all outstanding options within the director plan. Assuming the tender offer is well above the option price, this will be financially rewarding for the directors. The effectiveness of these provisions depends on the skill of the general counsel or legal advisors of the company, but generally speaking, the directors should get some money from a sale—even if they don't make a killing.

Another opportunity that may arise out of such a sale or merger is for the board member to be selected to continue on the board of the acquiring—or merged—company. The director then gets his package as a result of the sale, but also gets the opportunity to serve on a larger company board, with presumably even more benefits and rewards. (Other benefits and advice on how to respond to a director compensation package when it is offered are included in Chapter Nine.)

PERSONAL REWARDS

Exposure to new and different people is an immeasurable reward for service on a corporate board. If the board is functioning properly, and if the other members understand their role, you should become acquainted with some fascinating, bright people engaging in the highest level of decision making. You'll meet individuals who think in global terms, have a broad perspective, are excited about opportunities, competition, and building organizations, and have a unique outlook.

We all tend to get bogged down in the details of our life—and especially at work it is easy to get so focused on our current high-priority project that we forget to think outside the box. We often don't even consider how our particular project of the month—or week— fits into the bigger picture of the department, division or company.

Having the chance to step back, get away from the details and micro-managing compulsion many of us share, is a great opportunity. You can think longer term, talk in broader concepts, and interact with people with new and different perspectives.

> Service on a board is an opportunity to meet and interact with people of diverse backgrounds, from different industries, who are usually very bright.
>
> Donald O'Neill, former Vice Chair, Warner Lambert and board member of more than a dozen boards throughout his career.

We believe this is one of the most important rewards of board service. Our research convinced us that other directors agree.

The chance to meet a new group of peers who have their own incredible professional credentials and other significant interests is a lasting reward. It opens up a whole new world to you. One director we know is a master gardener, with amazing credits in landscape design and plant development. His passion for this hobby has become even greater than his passion for his banking business, and the sideline offers him another way to put business problems in perspective by understanding the nature of the seasons, long term growth, slow pollination, the beauty of persistency in the care and feeding of things, and the power of patience in waiting for results.

Other directors we served with have hobbies in fly fishing, taking them to remote lakes and rivers in place we've never heard of before. Others devote their life to special charities or efforts that give them a dimension that is richly rewarding, such as the director who helped co-found the Partnership for a Drug Free America, Jim Burke. This former chairman of Johnson and Johnson, and a member of many corporate boards in his life, claimed he worked harder for the Partnership than he ever worked for any company.

Other rewards include the opportunity to attend functions, engage in sporting events, and socialize with people who have unprecedented access to some of the finest aspects of American cultural life. Attending a fundraiser on the stage of the Metropolitan Opera isn't something ordinary folks often get to do, but by associating with other directors who had a passion for classical music, we were exposed to just such a once-in-a-lifetime experience.

Enhancing your professional skills and reputation, receiving annual cash retainers and stock option plans, broadening your perspective and accessing a new group of peers—all are examples of the rewards that make serving on a board worthwhile and enjoyable.

RISKS

So much for the upside. There is always a downside risk and board service is no exception. As you consider whether the boardroom is where you want to be, you must be realistic about the risks you will face. The primary risk is that you join the board of a company that proves to be unstable, poorly managed or ill-fated. This generates poor financial results or an unforeseen event triggers a public relations nightmare and legal action. (Think British Petroleum or Countrywide Financial for a moment...). A risk becomes a reality and you suffer damage to your professional reputation, your pocketbook or your personal calendar as a result of your board service. While it doesn't happen often, it is not as far-fetched as one might like to think, so let's take a look at each of these scenarios.

RISK OF DAMAGE TO YOUR PROFESSIONAL REPUTATION

We live in a period of unprecedented volatility in the lives of corporations and in the business and political landscapes in which they operate. Signing onto the board of a healthy company is no guarantee that it will stay that way. During recent years, more than two hundred fifty corporations disappeared from the listing of publicly traded companies. During the same period, roughly twenty-eight thousand companies worldwide have been acquired or merged. Anytime a significant event occurs in the life of a corporation the board is, or should be, intimately involved. A poor outcome can seriously tarnish the professional reputation of all involved.

Reputations plunge with share price?

Consider the case of Company X, conspicuously written up in the *Wall Street Journal* recently, where the directors sat on the sidelines as the CEO botched the possible sale of the company to a major financial house in 1999, and then saw the stock plunge from $76 in the spring of 1999 to less than $10 in the summer of 2001. They also ignored rumors about inadequate oversight of alleged payment for order flows, while they engaged in making profitable insider trades on their own. The general public probably doesn't care—or even know who these directors were. Unless the public is an investor in the company, it doesn't also care why the board didn't take action sooner against the CEO—a CEO who not only recruited each director, but was also the co-founder of the company.

There were thirteen members of the board. Seven of the directors were company employees or insiders; five members appeared to have been involved in the company first as an LLC before the initial public offering; some may have provided consulting services; only one appeared to be legitimately an outside independent director of the company. There were no women or minorities or individuals from outside the financial services industry on the board. One independent director out of thirteen is unacceptable by any standard.

Further, a corporate governance blunder was made when they combined the finance and audit committees. Normally, audit committees audit the financial transactions of the company and finance committees set financial plans and policy, and capital markets strategy. If both functions are performed within the same committee it is hard to imagine any degree of oversight or independence. It is somewhat like the FBI investigating itself.

For the financial community who followed this story, and for CEOs looking for possible new board members, having your name involved with this unfortunate incident would hardly be a recommendation for future service.

Even when a board is comprised of independent, seasoned directors with a broad range of experience, things can go wrong. An independent viewpoint and the Wisdom of Solomon are to no avail if time is not spent using them. When a public firestorm erupts in the blogosphere, on Twitter, or in the business dailies, it is often too late. Quarters ago, when the first signs of trouble began to appear, diligent directors should have begun the delicate process of encouraging the CEO to get a handle on things by not skirting the tough issues. Questions could have been asked that would penetrate these issues, challenged the accounting practices and got more relevant and comprehensive information to the directors.

No time to notice the warning signs before a big company goes bust?

A major technology hardware provider offers another classic case in reputational risk. The board was relatively small for the size of the company, with only six members. Including the Chairman, the six directors had twenty-eight other outside board seats among them. A recent Korn/Ferry study projects that it takes roughly one hundred seventy-six hours a year for each outside board assignment. Assuming that the study is correct, within a reasonable range, these directors already had committed four months of their time to other board seats– and that is without regard to any titles or positions they may have been holding as a fulltime job.

Historically, such well-connected directors would appear to be a plus, and their activity in other boardrooms would be considered another positive. But too much of a good thing is possible. From the perspective of the company's shareholders, whose interests the directors were to represent, one has to wonder if these overworked, overly well-connected individuals had either adequate time, or sufficient resources, to keep their eyes on the ball. Apparently not, as no one questioned the aggressive sales reporting practices that eventually led to the company's downfall.

Even when directors have ample time to adequately fulfill their duties of care, they may lack the distance and objectivity to fulfill their duties of loyalty and independence.

Did lack of independence contribute to these disasters?

This mid-size company had six board members, all of whom enjoyed their share of the limelight during the heady days before the Internet bubble burst. Surrounded by talk of eyeballs and search engines, digital communities and IPOs, it seemed as though no end to expansion was in sight.

In the midst of tremendous opportunity, it seems that the principles of good corporate governance were overlooked. The committee system was not used effectively. The audit committee, which met five times in 2000, was composed of only one independent non-employee. However, it now appears that even he was a former employee before becoming a director. The Strategic Opportunities Committee of the board did not meet at all. In the 20/20 vision of hindsight, this appears prophetic.

Three of the six directors were either current or former executives of the company. By no standard can this be considered an independent board. This once high-flying stock is now almost worthless, and thousands of shareholders are left holding the bag.

It may seem unfair. You join the board of a company that appears to be in good financial health, has a sound strategy, and apparently a bright group of professional managers. A few years go by, something unforeseen occurs, and suddenly you're in The *Wall Street Journal*, named in an article that you do not want to copy and send to your mother. We never said it was fair. It's a risk that you must weigh for yourself. You can greatly minimize the chance that board service will ever diminish your professional reputation by understanding your duties of loyalty, care and independence, by being prepared, being present and participating actively, and by choosing your affiliations wisely.

That's all any of us can do. Oh, and one more thing: don't create risk to your professional reputation where there is none. Read on.

Creating your own risk, or "loose lips sink ships..."

Reporters love to get ahold of inside information, and whenever there is the slightest clue that something is going wrong in a corporation, the business reporters start calling anyone and everyone they can find: officers, vendors, regulators, and, of course, board members.

Some time ago a major oil company was going through some painful allegations, even by their own senior officers, that a pattern of racial discrimination existed in the company. One senior director, who himself had been the CEO of a major company, agreed to talk to the press. Somehow, he ended up being quoted in the *Wall Street Journal* to the effect that the board often heard reports on the company's employment practices, and never heard about any discrimination practices.

He intended no harm. He probably even thought he was trying to help. The fact that he agreed to an interview was bad enough (a serious breach of boardroom etiquette as directors are not to act as spokespersons for the corporation), but to practically admit that the board had no idea what was going on played right into the plaintiff's brief—and made the director look completely out of touch and over the hill. He created tremendous damage to his own reputation, where there had previously been very little risk.

Stay away from the media—and stay away from the temptation to discuss a company's boardroom issues with someone outside the board. There can be only one spokesperson for a company—and it is rarely, if ever, a director. Directors shared numerous war stories with us of board members who spoke out of turn or confided in non-board members about the pending dismissal or resignation of the

CEO. In some cases the news got back to the CEO before the termination meeting. It's an ugly scenario when an obvious leak can be traced right back to the culprit. Again, you can create serious damage to a professional reputation and possible legal liability by being a big mouth. Not only does the director do irreparable harm to the relationship with the CEO—and other board members— it is also obvious to everyone who hears the story (and this stuff has very fast legs) that the director's name has become damaged goods on any list of potential new assignments.

RISK OF DAMAGE TO YOUR POCKETBOOK

The personal financial risks of board service can include un-reimbursed expenses, unpaid retainers or other cash compensation, a loss in value of your personal holdings of the company's stock, lost income you could have earned if you had not been spending your time on a corporate board; and the possibility of financial liability incurred as a result of being named in a regulatory action or a third-party lawsuit.

How do you get into that kind of trouble? Is there anything you can do to prevent it? Yes and no. Yes, you can greatly reduce the risk that board service could actually result in a personal financial loss by choosing your board affiliations wisely, asking the right questions up front, executing your duties responsibly, and insisting on proper levels of Directors and Officers Liability coverage. No, in the sense that, like all risks, it can be reduced but it cannot be eliminated.

Let's look first at the risks you can control by choosing wisely and acting responsibly (not getting paid or having the stock tumble). Then we'll take a look at the wild card—the legal risks that arise when any John or Jane Doe decides to sue.

NOT GETTING PAID

We did hear a few war stories of directors who were never paid their agreed upon (orally, of course) retainers, and never saw an attendance fee after the meetings. We believe this is rare, especially for an established, publicly traded stock. Now, if you are choosing to sit on a start-up company, anything is possible and everything has happened. You pay your nickel and you take your chances. Be aware that the promised fees may not always materialize; that is the reason you need to do serious due diligence about the company, the executives, and the other directors before you sign on. No one likes to spend time or effort and not get paid. With the proper approach to accepting your first seat, (see Chapter Nine) this should never happen to you.

If, in place of cash remuneration, you have accepted a package of stock grants or options, you have agreed to the risk of the marketplace. Stocks go up and stocks go down. There is always a risk that the wonderful stock options you got when you signed onto the board, and the stock grants you received annually as part of your compensation, can go south. However, if you choose the right company, and do your job as a director effectively, you should have a positive impact on the chances that the stock will go north—and you will reap the rewards.

Knowing exactly what is going to happen in the market—when to sell and when to hold—is tricky business. It is complicated by the many restrictions on directors and quiet periods during which they may not sell. It is highly unlikely that you will be able to time the market. Better to look at that stock as a long term holding or frosting on the cake and put it away for a rainy day. Years from now, when you are ready to leave the board, is the time to decide if the risk paid off.

If you are considering joining a very young organization, one that is pre-IPO or still funded by venture capital money, realize that the possibility exists that you may be asked to be of assistance if the company hits a cash flow crunch. Having to dip into one's own assets generated from other sources can be painful. Some start-up companies view their directors as angels—and feel it is perfectly appropriate to ask those directors to kick in large sums of money to keep the operation going. Peer pressure can be intense in these situations. Some directors found themselves agreeing to fund another round just because they couldn't stand to be the only one at the table who refused to ante up. Before accepting a seat on such a young organization's board, be crystal clear as to what they are likely to ask and what you are willing to give.

THE STOCK GOES DOWN

Trading restrictions on directors limit the opportunities for getting in and out of stock and they are a very serious business. The financial community loves to interpret insider-trading behavior and make grandiose predictions based on the meaning of a director's sale of a certain amount of stock at a certain time, regardless of individual circumstances. Stay very close to the general counsel and corporate secretary on this issue, and never trade unless that very day you have cleared the transaction with the appropriate executives.

Our advice is that you not consider stock in a company where you are a board member as anything other than a long-term investment. It simplifies your world. As long as you are serving on the board, you must believe in the company's long-term prospects, right? Then, what better place for your investment dollars?

Another area of intensifying regulatory risk is liability under the federal securities laws. Although most of the risk rests directly with the company and the officers signing the compliance and reporting documents, individual directors need to be aware that regulatory reviews and investigations can consume enormous amounts of time and add significant stress to your life. Examples of activity that could prompt regulatory review might be the misstatement of financial facts that materially affect the company, omissions of facts in connection with the offer or sale of securities, issues involving the audit committee or fraudulent activities, including accounting practices and insider trading.

THE WILD CARD—LEGAL ACTION

The financial risk exists that a judgment will be entered directly and personally against you as one of a group of individually named directors. This is truly a rare circumstance, but in these volatile economic times, plaintiff lawyers are looking for any possible defendant with a deep pocket. The risk of being named in a lawsuit because you were the director of a failed company is always a possibility.

Third party litigation is part of the fabric of American business—and there is no way you can successfully prevent someone from filing suit. Certainly a well-run company that has mechanisms in place to assess its performance and permit remedies will review alleged improprieties and help reduce the likelihood of third party litigation.

The most painful thing for directors is to somehow be suckered into a deposition where they take the time to prepare, and then appear, before an attorney to describe in detail what they remember about a particular event or board meeting five or more years ago. Hopefully, a good general counsel will protect the directors, but sometimes it is inevitable—and the painful deposition process occurs. Do your very best to avoid that circumstance. Destroy, in a routine and timely manner, all of the notes and materials that you have from each and every board meeting. If you don't have a shredder, get one. If the materials are particularly sensitive or confidential, return your copy to the corporate secretary who should make an appropriate record that you no longer have papers or materials in your possession.

As a director, periodically ask the general counsel to review the loss prevention procedures the company has in place to protect directors and officers against undue legal liability.

Some measure of protection can be had through director and officer liability insurance, commonly referred to as D&O coverage. As soon as the discussions begin to get serious about joining a board, you need to determine what insurance coverage is available. You must ask the question and get a written summary of the coverage from the corporate secretary or general counsel. No one should be expected to actually read the entire policy (we are talking about a lot of fine print here), but a summary will give you the salient facts about coverage limits, deductibles, and any bizarre exclusions.

In addition to the D & O coverage, you need to know what the company policy is on reimbursement of expenses and losses, and whether all company-related expenses can be indemnified and reimbursed.

The authors have never, personally, known of anyone who has suffered personal financial harm from board service, but the risk is definitely there.

Some optimists will ask if you can protect yourself by early resignation. In other words, once the stuff hits the fan, can't you just bail out and thereby protect yourself? The answer is no. Exposure and risk freezes at the moment the alleged disaster takes place, and your resignation after the fact won't remove your name from the director list at the time things began to unfold. If things have deteriorated to the point a lawsuit is likely, it is too late to bail out and protect yourself—because you were present at the time of the alleged poor decisions, mismanagement or whatever else was taking place.

DISRUPTION TO YOUR PERSONAL CALENDAR

There are serious legal risks to serving on a corporate board. You are responsible, and you can be held legally accountable for the activities of the corporation– even if it does not result in financial harm to you. If you are named in a suit, or the corporation is undergoing the intense scrutiny of a protracted defense against a serious claim of product liability, misconduct in the capital markets or a bankruptcy—clear your calendar. The next few months are going to be painful and time consuming. You may never have to write a personal check, but you may be forced to testify, forgo a vacation, miss other important meetings, and lose focus on your own business dealings. Each director who shared such an experience with us described it as highly stressful, intense and disruptive of their personal, business and family lives. It can get pretty ugly out there.

SUMMARY

It should come as no surprise that in the rarefied atmosphere of today's corporate boardrooms there are substantial rewards to be had—some accrue to your professional reputation, others are financial or personal in nature. Together, we have taken a clear-eyed look at the risks involved—which just happen to mirror the upsides professionally, financially, and personally.

Finalizing this equation of reward and risk is individual. You must weigh these factors for yourself and arrive at your own conclusions. To help you reach your decision, let's look next at the responsibilities and the duties involved, and the hard work that is required. We have found that due diligence and commonsense, applied during the process of accepting a board seat, go a long way toward mitigating any undue risks. Once seated, if you concentrate on what you can contribute to the board, we think you'll get your just rewards.

2

RESPONSIBILITY AND DUTY

> What does it mean to be an independent director representing the interests of the company's shareholders, rather than your own? I think very few first-time directors have any idea….
>
> John M. Steel, Partner, DLA Piper

Board service is a long-term commitment to a company to perform a serious fiduciary responsibility. You serve on behalf of that company by participating as one of several members of the legally constituted board of directors. Every business that organizes as a corporation, in any of the fifty states, has the requirement to manage the company under the oversight of a board of directors. The Securities and Exchange Commission and the listing organizations for publicly traded companies—the New York Stock Exchange, the American Stock Exchange, and the National Association of Security Dealers— have significantly added to the legal requirements for board membership. In addition, the passages of the Sarbanes-Oxley Act in 2002, and the Dodd-Frank Act of 2010, have significantly changed the landscape in the board room, expanding the duties and responsibilities of each director. Choosing to serve as a director now means more than knowing the rules: it means accepting the responsibility of corporate governance.

It is the responsibility of every member of the board to be prepared, to be present, and to participate fully in the effective governance of the corporation. To be prepared is not as simple as just skimming reports on an airplane before the meeting. A director must be prepared to exercise their legal duties—the duty of loyalty, the duty of care, and the duty of independence. To be present requires an act of personal commitment and attitude, in addition to what may be significant blocks of time. And to participate will surely mean service on one of the many standing or ad hoc committees of the board.

Smart directors also inform themselves—and one of the key responsibilities of a director is to be informed and understand the implications of existing laws, regulations, and current court decisions. As you begin the process of your board candidacy, learn as much as you can about the new laws and regulations governing your targeted companies and their boards of directors. Most, if not all, public accounting firms make regular and frequent updates on Sarbanes-Oxley and Dodd-Frank developments available via webinar. In addition, there are numerous seminars held by directors organizations (such as NACD or the WCD) and many graduate schools (such as Kellogg at Northwestern, or the Rock Center at Stanford), which you should try to attend as part of your preparation.

> The responsibility of the board is in setting a strategy and supporting a culture, a system of values for the company that are the basis for all decision-making.... everything else is implementation. Debating both is a fair exercise.
>
> Jock Patton, former CEO, Rainbow Studies and board member of JDA Software, Hypercom and Swift Transportation

BE PREPARED

This is not the Boy Scouts. Or the Girl Scouts for that matter. A director must be prepared to act out of loyalty to the shareholders and stakeholders they represent, and to act with care, independent of their personal interests. That means being prepared for some tough decisions.

Duty of Loyalty

As a director, you have a duty of loyalty to act in the best interests of the shareholders of the corporation. You must balance this primary duty with the broader interests of the stakeholders of the company, which may include the employees, the suppliers, the customers, and the community. The interests of these stakeholders often conflict. You also must balance all of these interests against the personal relationships you develop with other board members, the CEO, and the senior management team. The decisions that result are often misunderstood and subject to criticism. The public and the financial press are free to second-guess the actions of the board and they often do so gleefully. No amount of pressure or pleading, however, can relieve you of your primary fiduciary responsibility to act out of loyalty to the shareholders of the corporation. It's defined as a matter of law. So, as the saying goes, if you can't take the heat, stay out of the kitchen.

It may sound simple, but is easy to get confused, especially if the CEO is the one who recruited you. As we shall see in later chapters, an invitation to join a board is often the result of a long-standing personal or professional relationship. In good times, this makes for an enjoyable atmosphere in the boardroom with a sense of camaraderie and mutual success. When times are hard and a company faces lay-offs, falling profits, or even a bankruptcy, the same place can become filled with tension and conflicting points of view.

How differently the shareholders at a large technology company, recently in the headlines, might feel if their directors had understood this distinction! Instead of being beholden to the CEO, and the senior director who recruited the CEO, the directors could have been questioning the astronomical quarterly results, exploring customer sales and accounting practices, insisting on an analysis of the continuous stream of asset write-ups and write-downs. Instead, the directors apparently believed their duty of loyalty was to the CEO and the lead (or senior) director. For too long, the directors sat silent, accepting whatever report was put in front of them. They did not exercise their responsibilities to the shareholders or the customers or the employees. The stock went into a freefall and lost almost ninety percent of its value in just a year. Thousands of employees have lost their jobs. Could the outcome have been different? Should the CEO have been held accountable and replaced months earlier? Or did the board make the right decision in supporting a bright, high profile executive during a difficult period?

This is a tough question to answer. The role of an independent director is to ask the tough questions. When things are going well in the company and it appears the CEO can do no wrong, no one wants to be the skunk at the garden party. But one of the primary responsibilities of a board is to make sure that management is performing appropriately and effectively executing the company's strategic and long-term business plans. If management is not performing, the board's job is to fire the CEO and hire a new one. Confusing personal relationships you may have with a CEO, and your duty of loyalty to the shareholders, only compounds the problem and often sets the stage for spectacular failure.

DUTY OF CARE

The responsibilities of a director include the duty of care. This duty is to act in good faith and to use ordinary, reasonable and prudent approaches in performing your fiduciary role with the company. Legally, that means you must be diligent in the performance of your duties. A director must always act in good faith, incorporating the basic attributes of common sense, practical wisdom and informed judgment as any other prudent person would in a like position under similar circumstances, all in the reasonable belief that the action taken is in the best interests of the company.

Courts often refer to actions performed in good faith as protected under the business judgment rule.

Essentially, a decision can be incorrect, but if the directors, in the process of reaching that decision, exercised their duty of care and performed reasonable due diligence in analyzing the issues involved, the court may not overturn the decision or hold the directors personally liable.

DIRECTOR INDEPENDENCE

One of the confusing aspects of director service is whether the director can and should be independent of the company. This is complicated by the common practice of referring to directors as insiders or outsiders. Let's set the record straight on this one.

For purposes of trading the securities of a company, the SEC classifies certain senior members of management and directors as insiders. This designation restricts their ability to trade in the stock while in possession of material information not widely disseminated among the public. Setting that broad description aside, a director may also be labeled an insider if he or she is an employee of the company. For instance, the CEO or CFO may sit on the board. Insiders, by definition, are not independent. They cannot be independent because they rely on the company to pay their salary. They have a vested interest in the decisions that are made and cannot divorce their personal impact from their professional judgment. Nor are they expected to.

But you are considering joining the board of a corporation as an independent, outside director. This implies the responsibility to remain independent and impartial during your service. You will be entering an arena where business is often conducted privately, behind closed doors. It may seem as though no one would know if you had a conflict of interest, or were tempted to act on your own behalf. Nothing could be further from the truth. A daily glance at the business journals or CNN reveals a landscape rife with interlocking directorates and potential conflicts of interest. Tread carefully.

This duty of independence means that a director should not use the company's information, resources, or connections for personal gain. And yet, almost every director we spoke with mentioned the benefit of expanding their circle of professional contacts and influence in their community or industry as being a direct benefit of board service. Confusing? It can be. Let's add just one more concept to help clear things up—private and confidential. The director should not use the *private and confidential* information, resources or connections of the company for personal gain. If, as a director, you are privy to the board's discussion of a potential acquisition of one competitor by another, can you call your broker and buy some stock on the way to the airport? Of course not. That would be trading on private information for your personal gain. If a week later that same competitor made an announcement to the trade press of the impending acquisition, then it has become public knowledge and you are as free to trade that stock as anyone else.

Smart directors not only avoid conflicts of interest, they impose an even higher standard on themselves: they avoid even the appearance of a conflict of interest. Personal integrity is a precious thing and we believe you should protect yours at all costs. So, if you are hoping that service on the board of a particular company, in a particular industry is going to create an unfair advantage for you and your business—forget it.

Let's address two other areas where directors frequently encounter questions about independence—providing consulting services and representing special interests.

PROVIDING CONSULTING SERVICES

If you are acting as a consultant to a company and now you have an invitation to join their board of directors, make a decision. Do you want to remain a consultant or do you want to go on the board? We do not recommend doing both. For some professions it may even be an outright violation of their ethics code to do both.

A technology consultant called in to undertake an e-commerce implementation would have a difficult time looking objectively at other alternatives that may jeopardize their project (and income). While the Securities and Exchange Commission has established detailed definitions of what independent really means, individuals should avoid the dual roles of consultant and board member with a company, regardless of their good intentions.

The decision to remain a consultant can be a very lucrative choice—and the mere fact that a company issues an invitation to join its board means they think highly of you and the work you are doing. Turn that endorsement into a marketing opportunity and spend careful time convincing the CEO of your gratitude for the invitation, your confirmation of the opportunity involved in joining a distinguished team of board members, and your wish that you could do both.

Then, either accept it or reject it. Make a choice. If you decide to remain a consultant, acknowledge the invitation and ask that the CEO refer you to another CEO who could benefit from the expertise you have to offer—either as a consultant or as a member of their board. Don't get trapped in the middle.

> One government affairs consultant who had billed considerable hours to a company made the decision to sacrifice her consulting status completely in order to join the board. Financially she lost substantially all of the fees her firm was generating from the company in exchange for the modest director compensation. But her rationale was 1) if she refused, the CEO might take that as a personal rejection and that could endanger her continued consulting arrangement; 2) the exposure to the other CEOs on the board and more government affairs departments could yield much more than the fees being sacrificed from this company; 3) there was no reason to expose herself or her firm intentionally to possibility of potential conflicts or ethical questions; and 4) she was ready to move on in her career—and in her firm—to new territory.

Refusal to accept an invitation to join a board can turn into a disaster. Some CEOs—who have notoriously huge egos—take any rejection personally. Toss in gender issues, and you can create an explosive circumstance conjuring up all of the earliest rejection memories for a male or female CEO. So tread lightly and gently over the rocky road of rejection. One expert claims the only safe reason for turning down an invitation is to state that your present workload is too heavy to allow you to make another commitment.

Any other reason can lead you down a path that could become a dead end.

Carefully consider each offer to serve, but save yourself untold trauma and tension by adopting a personal code of ethics that prohibits board service to a business where you are currently a provider of products or services.

REPRESENTING SPECIAL INTERESTS

Special interests are commonplace in the boardroom. Venture capitalists, major creditors, suppliers or bankers may be found on the board of thousands of public companies. Many CEOs think it is a good idea to recruit other CEOs onto their board. They think it is an even better idea if those individuals are the CEOs of companies that do significant business with their company. The result should be a board member that knows your business, a stronger customer relationship, and shared interests. This thinking is similar to the old real estate theory that the buyer and seller have the same interests at heart: transferring the property, right?

No matter the personal integrity of the individuals involved, board members who come to the table with special interests, special constituents, and special agendas have a very difficult time being effective board members.

If you are a large borrower at the local bank, and also serve on the board of the bank, you are trying to serve two masters. There are age-old lessons, starting with Hebrew law, that tell us it is impossible to serve two masters. Many of the banking debacles of the early 1980s involved cases where the major borrowers were also the major influencers on the board. Saving yourself and your own business will always be paramount. In the case of the credit unions and banks, it was the small depositors and the Resolution Trust Fund (e.g., you and me—the taxpayers) who suffered the consequences.

Nonetheless, it is common practice. Many CEOs think a major supplier, who has the success of both companies at heart, will be a great addition to the board. When questions arise or the blame game starts over the quality of parts (consider Ford and Firestone issues for just a moment), common interests always take a back seat.

One last word of caution for our readers with a law degree: often lawyers will perform legal services while sitting as a board member. This is rarely a good idea. Just the nature of representing a company as general counsel means you are analyzing activity, assessing legal risk, and assuring appropriate compliance in a way that is different from the approach that should be taken by a board member. If you are not serving two masters, you are certainly trying to serve one master with two different hats—a juggling act at best and a possible disaster at worst. The only way to make this work is if the lawyer is from a big enough law firm that a "Chinese wall" can be constructed so the board member is shielded from the work done by associates on behalf of the company. The Securities and Exchange Commission has set forth careful definitions of what is a potential conflict, and strict adherence to those guidelines is a must. The personal preference of the authors is to avoid this circumstance completely. There are enough law firms and board seats to go around, permitting everyone to serve without conflict or the appearance of conflict.

It has not been our intent to give you a comprehensive legal analysis of what your obligations are as a director, but any company that is seeking your services as a director should give you a good overview. Any company worth joining should have an orientation session that includes a briefing from the corporate secretary and/or general counsel on your duties of loyalty, care and independence. Insist upon it.

BE PRESENT

It's not enough just to show up at the meetings. Boardroom protocol dictates that you come to the meeting prepared. You must be prepared to exercise your duties—the duty of loyalty, the duty of care, and the duty of independence—with regard to the issues at hand. To be present requires an act of personal commitment and attitude, in addition to what may be significant blocks of time. Preparation is what you do before you show up; being present is what you do while you are there. We want you to know how much time is involved and what it means to be present in a way that supports the CEO and the management team, and creates an atmosphere of respect and a productive working environment.

How much time? One rule of thumb for board meetings is the old collegiate ratio of preparation time to class time: three to one. So for every hour of meeting time, you probably should figure on three house of preparation. That means reading all of the materials sent to you by the company, seeking additional information from the executives if you need it, scanning daily newspapers and blogs for news of the industry and competitors, checking the websites and industry journals to see what else is happening, and developing your own personal context and perspective on the business. Some materials are easy and fun to read; others are complicated financial documents where you must not only read the lines, but also read between the lines to decipher exactly what is being said. Can you skimp on this? If more board members had been paying attention to the financial statements sent to them by the CEO of Sunbeam, would the accounting irregularities have been discovered earlier and some of the losses avoided?

Do you have to go to all those meetings? Yes. You must make the time available to attend all of the board meetings. The Securities and Exchange Commission reporting rules require that your name appear in the annual proxy statement of the corporation if you do not attend at least seventy-five percent of the meetings—a very embarrassing way to get your name in print. You need to understand when and where board meetings are scheduled and how often, including special sessions or emergency meetings. While years may go by with nothing more than four routine, quarterly meetings, you must make yourself available for the unexpected—the sudden resignation of the CEO, a hostile take-over attempt, or a massive product liability event.

Supporting the CEO

As long as the CEO is the CEO, you must provide your support, your counsel, and your wisdom. The trick is to provide support while still thinking critically, and analyzing activities independently. Questions in front of the other members are always encouraged, and should be designed to promote candid discussion, surface alternate ideas, and explore all potential consequences of particular decisions. To the extent possible, your questions should be probing, but positive in tone.

If comments, or concerns, aren't adequately addressed in the boardroom, the sophisticated director should bring the issue to the CEO outside the boardroom—staying after the meeting, or phoning later, creating the space for a private discussion.

It takes time to develop a confident and candid relationship with a CEO. Never give any indication that, as a board member, you are not supporting the CEO—even while disagreeing with a particular idea. Those clues are best conveyed privately—always.

BE A CHEERLEADER FOR MANAGEMENT

In most companies, other members of senior management eventually surface in the boardroom to present reports, read slide show scripts, answer questions, and generally provide detailed information to the board. These are usually occasions of significance to the employee, so a great deal of preparation and forethought may have gone into their presentation.

Whenever possible, provide positive feedback to these individuals. Ask supportive questions, seek clarification, suggest other resources, and demonstrate that you are paying close attention to their efforts. Even if you doubt their credibility, question their materials, or think they may be incompetent, do not badger, embarrass, or undermine the individual in front of the board. These are the members of your CEO's team—and they should be given the deference and respect due to any team member.

If other board members grumble inside the boardroom about management, don't join in the maligning; simply try to offer explanations and balance to the discussion. But, the CEO must be made aware of these concerns as soon as possible. Every CEO has to support their management team, most CEOs are slow to see defects in their hiring choices, and all CEOs will appreciate your tact in the boardroom. Your personal feelings should always be shared privately with the CEO—as it may be just the added insight that will prompt him to act.

In summary, bring your pom-poms into the boardroom. Create an environment that is supportive and elicits open discussion. Greet members of management when they enter the room, congratulate them on their presentation, and praise their efforts. When appropriate, offer constructive suggestions for improvement.

RESPECT THE OTHER MEMBERS

The group dynamics of any board are significantly changed when a new member joins. Hopefully, the change is for the better.

New members need to pay particular attention to their colleagues on the board: who they are, how long they have been there, why they were recruited, what their relationship is to the other members and to the CEO.

While deference is an old-fashioned term, at least in the beginning, new directors need to defer to the senior members, in terms of experience and age. Listen to what they say, learn from the questions they ask, and develop a rapport with each of them, both during the meetings and at every opportunity outside the boardroom.

An atmosphere of mutual respect among the members of the board allows each director to contribute fully and increases the effectiveness of the corporate governance process. Don't weaken this process unintentionally by pursuing a personal agenda inside the boardroom. Some individuals believe that they have a passionate cause that everyone should adopt or that they have a parochial position that should be advanced.

Just don't bring it into the boardroom.

One director we knew believed that a particular member of management was unfit for service in the company. He may have been right, but it was unseemly, if not downright destructive, to push that opinion in the boardroom. Let the CEO hear about your concerns in his or her office—alone. This gives the CEO the opportunity to pursue the matter further with other board members.

Other directors have been known to insist on certain employment practices or public relations campaigns or special community activities. Board members are not recruited so that they can get involved with the nitty-gritty detail of running the business, making management decisions, choosing vendors, funding local activities, or advancing social agendas. If you want to do that, run your own business. There are plenty of forums for this kind of activity. The corporate boardroom is not one of them.

Admittedly, it would be naïve not to acknowledge that the pursuit of personal agenda does go on. Just remember the efforts of a noted mega board member, Vernon Jordan, to find an appropriate position for one Washington, DC intern. Our general rule is don't do it. It puts undue pressure on the organization and can possibly be a source of personal embarrassment to the board member.

PARTICIPATE

You're prepared. You're present. Now you must participate. Of course, you will attend and comment during the full sessions of the board, but for most directors, the real work gets done in the committee. Our research shows that you can do your best work within your assigned committee. Talk with the chair of the Nominating and Governance committee early on about which committee you think you can serve the best. In some companies these assignments are rotated, but try to start with the committee that is focusing on areas within your expertise.

Some boards work very effectively through the committee system, and some prefer to do most of their work in front of the full board. The number of committees, and their sophistication, often increases with the age and market capitalization of the organization, but not always. A public company such as Anheuser-Busch has nine committees, while another public company, Nucor, has only one. Let's take a look at the most common committees you many encounter:

AUDIT

All boards have at least one committee: the Audit Committee. Members of this committee are expected to monitor: operational and strategic risk in the corporation; the integrity of the system of internal controls and the resulting financial statements; the qualifications and independence of the external auditors; the performance of both the internal audit function and the work of the external audit team; and the company's compliance with a myriad of laws and regulations. This is quite the workload.

Some consider it the best committee for a newcomer to the board, as you learn the inner workings of the company, the details of the various operations and possible soft spots. Others feel its members should be more senior and experienced. The Audit Committee should have only independent directors as members. New rules adopted by The New York Stock Exchange and the Securities Exchange Commission require each member of an audit committee to be financially literate, and to have at least one member of the audit committee with accounting or related financial management expertise. Each board of directors makes the business judgment as to exactly what independent and financially literate means.

At a minimum, the member needs to be able to read financial statements, understand the basics of accounting controls and procedures, and have the capacity to ask hard questions about the details of any particular audit report. This committee requires a lot of work and participation and can present risks above and beyond the normal director risks. Given recent SEC pronouncements, the significance of the Audit Committee cannot be emphasized enough.

COMPENSATION

This committee oversees the compensation package for the CEO, the policies and procedures for compensation and benefits for the company, and director compensation. Some expand their responsibilities to include management development and succession planning. While some human resource knowledge and expertise is probably helpful, common sense goes a long way in the compensation committee discussions—and is something many boards could use.

As noted in a recent article by Pay Governance LLC, "The responsibilities associated with serving on the compensation committee of a company's board have increased significantly in recent years with the enactment of the Dodd-Frank Wall Street Reform and Consumer Protection Act of 2010 and mandated "say on pay", governance reform and enhancements, and increased shareholder activism. With the increasing complexity of the executive compensation landscape, effective management of the ongoing operation of the compensation committee has become increasingly challenging."

If this is to be your initial committee assignment, you will want to attend training to ensure you are up to speed with the new requirements and have a thorough understanding of the company's compensation plans. This can be an educational committee for service, and generally there are no more than four meetings per year, usually less.

NOMINATING & GOVERNANCE

This committee oversees the general operating practices of the board of directors, reviews committee and director performance, and has responsibility for nominating new directors. This is an opportunity to learn about the board, and a potential opportunity to influence, in significant ways, the future of the company and the board of directors. Generally, this committee meets only two or three times a year—and unless the recruitment needs are significant, the work is pretty even and manageable.

OTHER COMMITTEES

It is not uncommon for companies to create committees for special purposes or discrete assignments. The Executive Committee is such an example. It was originally designed to act when it was not possible to convene the entire board. Now, with modern video and teleconferencing technology permitting board meetings on a moment's notice, it may have outlived its usefulness. Finance

Committees are used by some corporations to set financial policy and oversee long-term budgeting and financial operations. Corporate Public Policy and Environmental Affairs Committees, such as the one at SBC Communications, Inc., oversee public activities and assure compliance with the numerous environmental activities of the company.

©Mark Litzler. Used by permission.

LITZLER

"Even for a new board member it's a bummer of a committee assignment."

In addition to these standing committees that may continue year after year, some companies use ad hoc or interim committees to explore particular issues, such as international expansion, customer service in a crises, compliance reviews, credit crunches or the phase-out of a product line. All are generally short-term assignments, but they can nevertheless be intense, complex, and time-consuming.

The number and names of committees is only limited by the imagination of the CEO and their board members. The important point is to find a committee where you can contribute your knowledge and experience, actively participating in the process of effective corporate governance.

SUMMARY

The boardroom is not for everyone. It carries with it a significant burden of responsibility, duty and commitment. It is the obligation of every member of the board to be prepared, to be present, and to participate fully in the effective governance of the corporation. Sounds like all work and no play, doesn't it? Actually, it can be very heady stuff. Exciting. Challenging. And now that you understand the risks, rewards, and responsibilities involved, you're ready to learn more about what CEOs are looking for from their directors.

3

ACROSS THE TABLE: PERSPECTIVES FROM THE CEO

> This is not a spectator sport.
>
> Larry Downes, CEO, New Jersey Resources

The CEO is a unique member of the board of directors. By definition, the position is not independent or without conflict. CEOs are deeply involved with every aspect of the company's performance and judged not only by the ability to see the big picture, but also by the ability to deliver quarterly results to the bottom line. The CEO is the primary relationship, the hub that connects each of the other directors to the board. Often, it was the CEO's decision to offer a seat on the board in the first place. The board can offer advice and influence the direction of the business, but the CEO does not have to accept their help. The relationship developed and tested over the years by the challenges of the business cycle, can be one of deep trust and professional respect; or, it can become bitter, acrimonious, and adversarial. The board can fire the CEO: the CEO cannot fire the directors.

How it all turns out is as individual as the person holding the position.

Because this relationship is so central, so primary to every director, we wanted to start by examining how things look from the other side of the table. We'll take the emphasis off of your anticipated role as a new director, and focus instead on what the CEO that recruits you is thinking. Then, in Chapter Four, we'll contrast this CEO perspective with that of the seasoned director revealing an inherent conflict and tension that is part of the dynamic of corporate governance.

> *Inherent conflict... sounds like the boardroom is a negative place?*

Not at all. Conflict and tension are necessary to the integrity of any healthy structure—think of the system of checks and balances among our three branches of American government. Certainly the judiciary, the legislative, and the executive branches are often in conflict, but it is a necessary tension that allows for a systematic (if at times, grindingly slow) balancing of the needs and wants of a large electorate.

A similar process takes place every day between the forces of the marketplace, the CEO (representing the company and its employees), and the members of the board (representing the shareholders). The roles are different, the duties are different, and the resources and powers assigned to each are unique.

What does a board look like from the vantage point of the CEO? What are the criteria for selecting a candidate to fill an open seat? Our interviews gathered some wide-ranging opinions with many of the CEOs disagreeing with their counterparts. They are a diverse, strong-willed group and so we expected that. We can summarize their responses for you into four broad areas:

- As a CEO, I want my directors to bring me the skills and experience that I don't already have

- I want them to get along with me and the other members of my board

- I want them to tell me what I need to hear, and what I don't want to know

- I don't want them to make me crazy

BRING ME SKILLS AND EXPERIENCE

I look for someone who can really add value, who has some seasoning, with P&L experience. I want someone who can empathize with my role as the CEO because they have done it themselves. My best directors were themselves current CEOs and knew what I was facing every day.

Former public company CEO in the Southwest

CEOs generally look first for a director that has good commercial judgment, as evidenced by their successful track record in running a business, with high integrity. Then they look to add expertise in a specific area that they are lacking in or that represents a new direction for the company. For instance, if an organization is getting ready to expand overseas, the CEO may look for a director that has successfully accomplished such an expansion within his or her own company. If the business needs to gain scale quickly through a series of rapid acquisitions, the CEO is looking for a director with plenty of M&A (mergers and acquisitions) experience. The idea is to round out and fill in the skill gaps with each new addition, not to duplicate what the CEO already does or knows.

Many CEOs told us that the single most important skill of a director is their ability to think strategically. This thought process requires recognition, not fear, of risk; assessment of all the alternatives, and the courage to make a decision and take action, knowing that all decisions will not necessarily be right. It requires a confident CEO to work with a strong team of directors who can think and plan strategically.

Every CEO can benefit from the wealth of information and knowledge that the individual directors have gained through their participation in the business world. CEOs described that benefit as coming from advice given in a variety of ways—including written materials, quick telephone conversations, e-mails and texts. The advice can also be provided through a series of questions to the CEO, such as the simple "Have you thought of...?", through war stories of "This is what happened at our company...", or by referrals to other CEOs whose companies are grappling with the same issues.

No Mirrors here

Why have mirror images of who already works at the company or who is the current CEO? I've been on boards where all they did was talk to each other and say what everybody already knew. There's no value in that.

CEO, private multi-media company in the West

GET ALONG WITH ME AND THE OTHER BOARD MEMBERS

During an actual board meeting, it is not only what you know, but how you are able to communicate, that makes the difference between a significant contributor and an irritating know-it-all. That is why CEOs look for a director with good interpersonal skills and judgment in addition to their areas of expertise.

DON'T BRING AXES TO THE TABLE

What do I look for in a new board member? Well, first, that they get along well with the other members of my board. I want an atmosphere where we can work effectively together. No animosity, no one with an axe to grind.

Tim Crown, Chairman of the Board, Insight Enterprises

Board members must understand that they are not managing the company. They must know that it is their responsibility to work *with* the CEO, *with* the other board members, and work *through* the members of management to achieve results in a constructive way. This is teamwork at the highest level.

Hackett says the CEO wants respect most of all

According to Jim Hackett, CEO of Ocean Energy, ex-CEO of Anadarko, and member of multiple boards, professional respect is critical: respect from his directors, his respect of the directors, the directors' respect of each other and their respect for the company and the management team. This is an earned culture at the board level. It means everyone is candid and transparent with each other and competent at their respective roles. Any Board member or CEO who is missing these traits and skills must be removed as soon as practical. Shareholders depend on the Board to properly represent their interests and have no interest in further exacerbating the investment challenges that exist even when competent and candid Board members and CEOs are in place.

Jim goes on to point out that directors and CEOs need to have high integrity, good commercial judgment and be collegial. Board members have many options for service, and want to be with people they respect and feel are their partners in an important mission for the shareholders.

CEOs look for directors who have self-confidence, a winning style, a healthy mindset, and a perspective that permits them to share information appropriately, support others successfully, and contribute to a board-level discussion in a meaningful way.

CAN'T WE JUST BE FRIENDS?

The current de-emphasis on friendship, as an important consideration when selecting board members, is a big change from the way things were done over the past fifty years.

In the past, CEOs were often the sole source of recruitment activity so friendship and connections were the key criteria. "How well do I know the candidate, can I trust him, and will he be enjoyable company out on the golf course and at our board retreats?" were once familiar considerations.

Given human nature, we all choose to surround ourselves with people who have had common experiences, who think like us on a variety of topics, and, often, people who even look like us. Over the years we've noted that in some corporate boardrooms most of the executives and directors are tall, slender, good-looking men; in another boardroom most of the executives and board members belong to one particular ethnic group. In the early 1980s there were jokes about men who had that IBM look, or the Procter & Gamble or the American Express look.

But in the last quarter century we have seen numerous changes in the Good Old Boys Network. Now boardrooms are *somewhat* more diverse, but there is still much to be done. It is now more unusual for lifelong friends to be sitting at the table of a publicly traded company, although relatives may still be gathered in the boardroom of a family-owned business.

In smaller companies, there is often a very fine line between the CEO's buddies and the board members—even today. It is not uncommon for such a board to have the CEO, another member of management, a lifelong friend that the CEO trusts implicitly (perhaps a former professor, co-worker or boss), and one independent soul who brings in the financial expertise.

KEEP THE BUDDIES ON THE COURSE

> CEO chemistry and trust is essential, but golf buddies just don't belong in the boardroom. You can spot 'em a mile away. Friends compromise a director's necessary ability to make tough decisions...I've found that the more money there is at stake, and the more friends you have in on the deal, the more tension and acrimony you'll find in the boardroom. Friendships tend to dissolve as the stakes get higher.
>
> California-based venture capitalist and board member

Integrity was mentioned so often that it is clearly a key criterion. CEOs want and need directors who are trustworthy. Integrity had many definitions. One described it as a person who works well with others and can develop a sense of mutual trust among the other board members. Others suggested that integrity requires high moral principles based on the Judeo-Christian concepts of the golden rule: treating people right, being honest and forthright, caring for others with respect. Most agreed that one key way to judge a member's integrity was to watch the way that person reacts to a crisis—whether it be a major world crisis, a mistake in the financials or an inconvenience when travel plans suddenly change.

TELL ME WHAT I NEED TO HEAR, AND WHAT I DON'T WANT TO KNOW AND WHAT I WISH I KNEW

> The best directors make comments that make you uncomfortable, that really make you think. They are thought provoking, but, not provocative in their manner.
>
> Jeff McKeever, Chairman and CEO, MicroAge, Inc.

During the years of their relationship, the three most important things a CEO will hear from the individual board members often occur in a one-on-one meeting. These are: advice, confirmation and, when appropriate, a course correction.

A CEO needs affirmation. All of us need reassurance that we are doing the right things, have the right priorities, and are heading in the right direction. CEOs have that same need. While he or she can get some of that necessary confirmation from management (which may be suspect in its praise), some from the stock market, and a little from industry analysts or the press, the best affirmation comes from individual directors as they take the time and communicate privately to the CEO that they are on the right track.

CIVILITY AND COURTESY ARE STILL IN VOGUE

> The board has a duty of loyalty and respect to the CEO. Being a CEO is a lonely job, a tough job. You are always an agent of change—trying to get people to do what they don't want to do, or are not already doing… The CEO deserves diplomacy from the other board members. He's in a tough spot.
>
> Jock Patton, director of JDA Software,
> Hypercom and Swift Transportation

Private conversations are also used to convince CEOs (and others when appropriate) of what they don't want to know—that they need to do succession planning, for example, or of the need for a significant change in the company's direction.

One of the toughest—but most important—jobs for the board of directors is to hire and fire the CEO. A good board must constantly be engaged in the evaluation of the CEO and members of senior management. A good director will be pushing, persistently, for the succession planning process that has not been in evidence in many of our major companies recently. This failure to force the CEO to plan for succession is driven by the current popular practice of bringing in fresh blood. However, the success of those outside CEOs is very mixed, and there are few really great success stories.

The better approach is to be constantly looking *inside the company*, and outside, for the next CEO. The board should play a key role in that process. Two current examples of effective succession planning (that went on for years) have been found at General Electric and at American Express. As one sage director noted, it is better to deal with the devil you know than the one you don't.

Private meeting yields key career advice

One CEO recounted a series of meetings with a board member that had occurred while he was still the second in command at the company. A director sought him out and provided invaluable advice. His very survival as an executive, and his ultimate promotion into the position of CEO, were the direct result of these meetings. The director came to him outside the boardroom, spoke privately about his concerns for the company, and then supported him through coaching and mentoring.

It was a difficult board process when the sitting CEO was eventually asked to resign by the board. But the advance information and the individual coaching, advice and support received eventually led to an orderly and successful transition. Without that director's support, the board may have turned to an executive search firm and undoubtedly recruited someone from the outside—someone who did not know the company and could not have recognized its challenges, or implemented the necessary solutions, in such a timely manner.

Similarly, private conversations often clue the CEO into the fact that a correction in course is needed. Examples CEOs shared with us included realizing it was time to consider the replacement of the CFO, or to be more vigilant in the union negotiations, or to watch the sales and accounting practices in the foreign operations more carefully. All these were difficult discussions, but important conversations that needed to be held.

It is the strong, effective director who will take the time, and has the courage, to confront these issues and counsel privately with the

CEO. On other occasions, directors will have concerns that are not ripe enough to surface in the formal boardroom. A private conversation can be an opportune time to help the CEO identify and solve an operational issue or change a company policy, before it becomes a major problem and fodder for the front page of *Barons*.

Mature, confident CEOs appreciate a board member who has the courage to raise the need for an independent review of company activities if the situation, and the potential public relations debacle, call for such review. Many companies, including JPMorgan and Prudential, have had strong directors who understood they needed to protect themselves, the shareholders, the employees, the customers and other stakeholders by engaging completely independent consultants who conducted an investigation and reported directly back to the Board. This is a powerful tool—available only for times of true concern or crisis—and it takes a courageous director to tell a CEO this is what is needed.

AND DON'T MAKE ME CRAZY

CEOs had no problem articulating what it is about certain board members that drove them crazy: talking too much or doing too much.

One CEO vividly recounted his experiences with a director who was a futurist and a professor at a prestigious Eastern university. He told of countless meetings where this individual, lacking real-world business acumen, would go off on a tangent, testing out one of their new ideas for the next research project or the classroom. Professors are used to having fifty minutes of uninterrupted time to espouse their theories to a lecture hall full of captive students. It made this CEO "absolutely crazy".

This aggravating habit of talking too much can occur both in and out of the boardroom. We heard incredible stories of directors using loose lips to sink ships—usually their own. What goes on inside the boardroom stays there, and what a CEO tells a director in confidence must also stay with that director.

The former executive director of The National Association of Corporate Directors had a useful rule for keeping board members from doing too much. He called it "NIFO"—as in Nose In, Fingers Out. The ability to sense what is really going on —to sniff out the problems, to poke around in and challenge the strategies, accounting practices, or marketing plans without meddling, this is the balance a director must strive for. Members who over-reached, trying to dive into the day-to-day operations of the company and to micro-manage for results drove the CEOs we spoke with absolutely nuts.

SUMMARY

The CEO is in a unique position among the board members, and has his or her own perspective on what is needed, expected or wanted from each director. We can sum up how things look from this side of the table as follows:

- As a CEO, I want my directors to bring me the skills and experience that I don't already have

- I want them to get along with me and the other members of my board

- I want them to tell me what I need to hear, and what I don't want to know

- And, I don't want them to make me crazy.

PART II

THE DIRECTORS: DO YOU HAVE WHAT IT TAKES?

Have you now established, in your mind, what it is that board members really do, why they do it, and the central conflict that is inherent in their role? We've discussed the risk and the reward, the responsibility and the duty, and the perspective of the CEO. Are you still interested? Then let's find out what makes a good board member—and what, if anything, the two sides of the boardroom table have in common.

In the chapters that follow, you'll find out that the definition of a good board member changes with the situational needs of the company, the skills of the other directors on the board, and, to some extent, the temperament and abilities of the CEO.

You'll also be performing a self-assessment to determine if you possess the six qualifications common to almost every director as they take their first seat on a corporate board. And, you'll come to understand that being talented isn't enough—timing and positioning along the arc of your career path will also have a part to play.

4

WHAT MAKES A GOOD BOARD MEMBER?

> The best directors I've seen are the active CEOs because they're always tuned up, they're in the market every day. Of course, they're also the toughest ones to get. The good ones always tell you no the first time, they're too busy. But, keep asking.
>
> John Bauer, (former) Executive Vice President, Nintendo America Corporation; (former) director of Zones, Inc.

It's time to talk about what you can bring to the boardroom table, and about the directors who are already there. We start, in this chapter, by setting the benchmark against which you can measure your potential to get in the door, take a seat at the table, and make meaningful contributions. In our research, we repeatedly asked CEOs and directors to give us their observations on what distinguishes the exceptional directors from those who simply keep their chair pad warm. We want you to understand the wide range of contributions made by good board members. We'll also contrast that with several examples of negative or dysfunctional behavior that a board hopes to avoid when selecting its newest member.

Two characteristics generated widespread agreement: the ability to work well with the other members of the board and financial acumen. What else? Well, that depends on who you are asking, the size and health of their company, and what contributions other members of the board are already making.

THE ABILITY TO WORK WELL WITH OTHERS

The ability to get along with the other board members includes building a supportive relationship with the CEO. How the role of the board looks from the perspective of the CEO may be similar or vastly different from the way directors perceive their own roles. These differences can create fertile ground for disagreement and tension during a board meeting, especially if the added stresses of financial challenges or personal issues are present.

We'll see in later chapters that this quiet, difficult-to-describe attribute of getting along with others is the key to sitting down at the table.

What is required of a director is not that they be nice, easy-going or a yes-man. On the contrary, directors create considerable liability for themselves if they do not question the decisions of a CEO and blindly go-along just to get-along.

The best board member has these three attributes: they're an active participant, they understand the business, and they're a good compromiser—they can move the other board members and the CEO forward towards agreement.

Dan Eitingon, President, Legacy Capital

What is required of a director are skills in fact-finding, human nature, and consensus building. Every board appreciates those members who can calmly, and without blame, determine the relevant facts necessary to make an informed decision.

Style is important for directors…constructive questions are best, where the director can ask a strategic question that is focused on the issues…and cheerleading sounds superficial, but it is very important to the CEO and management.

John (Jay) Cowles III, former Chairman of the Board, Cowles Media Co.

The effective director, after reading the personal, human nuances of the situation, makes a determination as to whether the company's interests would best be served by an immediate vote, waiting to get more information, or taking the issue "off-line" to allow for some one-to-one conversations that can build the consensus necessary to go forward with a unanimous vote of the board.

This is the type of rational, mature, fact-based decision-making and interpersonal skill that is meant by getting along with the other members of a board. It's easy to see why that is an attribute everyone can agree on when describing what makes a good board member.

FINANCIAL ACUMEN

> Financial acumen is absolute table stakes or you will not be able to contribute effectively as a board member. This does not mean that you have to have been a CFO; rather that you have had your own experience operating a company or running a large division with P&L responsibility and budget authority.
>
> William Keiper, (former) director, JDA
> Software Group, Inc., Zones, Inc.

What is meant by financial acumen? What, exactly, does a director have to be able to understand when it comes to financial statements? At an absolute minimum, a director must understand the fundamentals of a balance sheet, a P&L (profit and loss) statement, cash flow (sources and uses of cash), footnotes, an audit opinion, and the capital and operating budget process.

Before each meeting of the board, a board package is usually sent to the directors. Although some boards may still deliver a package in hard-copy, most now use a board portal. This drop-box is password protected and allows you to view confidential information online. Management can post and update information frequently. Directors can review and bring along the entire digital package on their tablet or other device.

In addition to an agenda, minutes from the prior board and committee meetings, and some background information about topics to be discussed, the package will include the financial statements for the company. These might be for a quarter or for a month, or if this is the annual meeting of the shareholders, for an entire fiscal year. Challenges and issues in other areas may come and go, but a review of the financial results are a part of every board meeting.

> Each director has to come in the boardroom ready to contribute something of value: personal experience, knowledge, financial keenness, and connections that will add substance to the work of the board.
>
> Len Coleman, former President of the National League and Major League Baseball and board member of several publicly traded companies

A director is expected to review these statements prior to attending the meeting. This may take an hour or several hours, depending on the complexity of the company. After this review, the director should be able to participate in a discussion of the company's financial health. This requires a basic understanding of what a healthy current ratio should be, whether the cash position seems sufficient, if revenues are lagging behind the growth reported by competitors, if sales, general operating or manufacturing costs are too high, if inventory days on hand seems to make sense or if expenses are increasing at a faster rate than revenues, causing margins to shrink.

During the meeting, the CFO or controller will often present the statements and discuss the period's results. That is the time for questions and probing at trends and underlying issues by the board. It is not the time for a tutorial on how vendors could have a credit balance in accounts receivables or what is meant by amortization of goodwill. A board member must come to the role with this basic understanding of the fundamentals of corporate accounting, finance, and the budget process.

However, a director is not required to be an expert. Rather, the requirement is to understand the basics, to have been exposed to enough budgets and annual reports and tax returns that you know a problem when you see one, and to have the wisdom to confer with experts or request additional information when appropriate.

For example, when a change is proposed to GAAP (generally accepted accounting principles), the AICPA (American Institute of Certified Public Accountants) or the SEC (Securities and Exchange Commission) will issue a series of discussion drafts and policy statements before the change is adopted. It would be common to have the independent auditors of the company come in and make a brief presentation to the board, informing them of the changes and discussing the anticipated effect they would have on the company's financial reporting. Board members are not expected to keep up with this on their own, unless they are in the accounting profession, but they are expected to have the background to understand the discussion and to contribute to a meaningful conversation about the effect and the options the business has to choose from.

An exception to this basic requirement for financial acumen is membership on the audit committee where the standards are higher. The New York Stock Exchange, the National Association of Securities Dealers, the American Stock Exchange and other organizations have adopted new requirements for audit committee membership. Except for very small-cap companies, audit committees now must have at least three members who are financially literate independent outsiders. For all companies, the audit committee needs one member who has financial expertise. Financial literacy means the ability to read and understand fundamental financial statements including a company's balance sheet, income statements and cash flow statements. Financial expertise means all of the above plus past employment in finance or accounting and requisite professional certification or other experience that result in financial sophistication. This change has caused many boards to add new members who specifically have these heightened financial skills.

After agreeing on the ability to get along with other board members and possessing financial acumen, what makes a good director depends on the unique situation of an individual company. Opinions expressed by the CEOs and directors we interviewed varied widely based on their own experiences. We can group their responses, roughly, by the organization and size of their business as well as the phase of growth or type of challenges it is facing. These intersections, (illustrated in the following table) generated some basic agreements on what characteristics or skill sets would make a good board member for companies at that stage of their life cycle.

Requirements of Directors as a Function of the Corporation's Life Cycle

Type of Company	Start-up/ New	Rapid Growth	Maturity	Distressed
Privately held	Hands-on Time intensive Contacts Investors	Specialization such as legal, human resources, accounting or marketing	Broad experience, M&A experience, knowing when to sell	Legal, bankruptcy, exit strategy, M&A Corporate finance
Pre-public	Prior IPO experience, Investment Banking, Venture Capital Hands-on Time intensive Contacts	Specialization such as legal, human resources, marketing, and GAAP accounting/ auditing and systems	Broad experience, industry knowledge,	Legal, bankruptcy, exit strategy, M&A Sources of additional funding Corporate finance
Public	Investor relations, contacts with financial community Hands-on Time intensive	Specialization such as legal, human resources, marketing, and GAAP accounting/ auditing and systems	N/A	Legal, bankruptcy, exit strategy, M&A Sources of additional funding Corporate finance
Mature, public	N/A	N/A	Broad industry experience, M&A, R&D, new product intro, life cycle management	Legal, bankruptcy, exit strategy, M&A, corporate finance

The first differentiator is whether the company is private or publicly held. If the company is currently private, with the express purpose of going public in the next one to three years, then it is "pre-public". The distinction is important.

A privately held company, with no intention of going public, has far fewer regulatory and reporting requirements. It is not subject to the same whims of the public markets, and may not be scrutinized as closely by industry analysts and pundits. It can be a relief, and even a competitive advantage, to be able to make investment decisions or to enter new markets without the glare of the media and quarterly reporting. However, private companies may pose their own special challenges to the board. They may be closely held by a few members of the same family. Succession planning can be an emotional and difficult issue. The board must address key-man insurance and plan for the unfortunate possibility that the owner dies or is disabled.

We heard from several sources that to be effective in a privately held family company the majority of the board members should be outside the family, the chair duties should be separate from the CEO duties, and the directors must have the courage to ask constructive questions that lead the family members to think creatively and to acknowledge gaps in information.

Family members, investors or friends may dominate the board of a private business. Outside directors may find themselves in the minority, unable to form a coalition willing to rationally address exit strategies or evaluate the performance of executives who are also family members or long-term employees. Without access to the capital markets, additional financing may be difficult to raise and the business may be unable to grow.

Beyond those distinctions, both private and publicly held businesses evolve over time, passing through common stages of conception, rapid growth, and maturation; or they become distressed, going through a difficult period of recovery or ceasing to exist altogether. At each stage, the board membership may also change and evolve, requiring the addition of new members with skills appropriate to the current challenge. Existing members may need to make a graceful exit, realizing that they have made a substantial contribution, but it's time to move on.

STAGE: START-UP/NEW

Directors accepting a board seat for a new company are aware that the assignment will be more time intensive and hands-on, compared with more mature organizations. Often, these directors are expected to have significant contacts in the business community that represent actual prospects for the product or services of the new company, and often they are asked to aggressively solicit customers. They may be offered a seat on the board in exchange for a significant personal financial investment of seed or "angel round" money; or they may be the representatives of a venture capital firm that has made a first or second round investment in the new business. If the company is pre-public or newly public, they may be chosen for their contacts in the investment banking community and their relationships with analysts that follow similar stocks.

> It's fun to be on the big boards, but the new, younger boards are where you get the real joy of giving back.
>
> Carolyne K. Davis, former board member of
> seven publicly traded companies

Companies in this first stage also look for directors with human capital networks and experience. They expect to benefit from your significant relationships with executive search firms and your ability to open doors or arrange interviews with potential executives, law firms, audit partners, and commercial real estate brokers if leasing space is an issue.

Strange, but true...A privately held electronics firm in California is profitable, stable, and has a manufacturing process that basically runs itself. Their issue? They have no direct sales force and rely solely on the telephone and Internet-based sales efforts of their distribution partners. Their outside board members? All famous name athletes and coaches. They rely on these celebrity board members to go out and glad-hand the troops manning the telephones and calling on customers, asking them to purchase the electronic components made by the company.

STAGE: RAPID GROWTH

As a business survives those initial years of struggle and establishes itself as a survivor and a competitor, the demands on the board begin to shift. No longer a beginner without infrastructure or resources, the company now has established a management team and a way of doing things. The challenge? Most likely, the team that got them to this point is not the right team to carry them through a period of rapid growth and expansion. The way they have of doing things has probably worked just fine up until now. But suddenly, instead of one hundred folks who all know Jane in shipping and can call her to get an order out, the company now has thirteen offices in six states and needs a computerized system that prioritizes shipments by customer and weight and integrates seamlessly with UPS and FedEx. Uh-oh.

> Once we moved from the development of product to the possibility that the company might actually be profitable, we needed a new set of skills in the boardroom. We needed sales expertise, marketing knowledge.
>
> John M. Seibert, CEO, CIMA Labs Inc.

Now begins a period of specialization and the demise of the generalist, the know-it-all who has been part of the management team since day one. The same holds true of the board. Now an open seat is filled by someone familiar with the industry and with a systems background or by someone with an expertise in franchising, real estate or legal issues. After those first few law suits, companies decide to establish policies and procedures, create a corporate culture supported by training and a hiring process, and place a human resources professional on the board. Time to build the brand? Expand your integrated digital marketing strategy. An executive from RazorFish or BrandRepublic will fill the next seat. Establish a presence on social media? Sponsor a major sporting event to gain exposure for the business? An executive from Proctor and Gamble or a partner in an advertising agency out of San Francisco or New York, fills the next board seat.

> After we went public, things changed. One by one, the guys who got us there—the investors, the banker—cashed in and rotated off. What do I want from my board, now? I want them to add value with opinions and contacts and perspectives that I don't have. It doesn't help me to sit around and talk to myself. When we run into a problem, or the first time we set out to do an acquisition overseas, these guys knew just who to call. They had done it before, with the right attorney, the right investment bank, they just picked up the phone. I don't expect them to bring in new business or call on my customers—I can do that myself. But find me something faster or better than I could have done—save me time, save me money, save me from a costly mistake. That's what my board is good for.
>
> CEO, public distribution company in the southwestern US

STAGE: MATURITY

Things change. Now the company is no longer growing by leaps and bounds. Perhaps internal problems, or inefficiencies that have been covered up by years of double-digit growth, begin to rear their ugly heads. Complacency sets in because the company continues as the market leader. The economy goes into recession; a young upstart eclipses a major product line. Maturity has its own set of challenges.

Now a good board member may be one who has steered his or her own business through this cycle. Instead of the risk-taking investor with seed money that a company courted as a start-up, now the right candidate has wisdom, finesse, and, more than likely, a few gray hairs. A sense of history is required if the questions of the day are "How long will this recession last? Should we close the plant in Detroit? Lay off the third shift in Taiwan? Is now the time to sell a division to a competitor and raise needed capital to feed our growing lines of business? What if we dig in and try to just wait this thing out?" These are the times when a business wants practical, sage advice from patient executives who have been there and done that and lived long enough to cash in their options.

STAGE: DISTRESS

Some companies may pass successfully through a period of genuine risk and distress where the possibility of ceasing to exist looms large. Others seem to live on this brink of failure perpetually. Most companies will experience real threats to their existence at some point in their corporate life cycle—bankruptcy, a hostile takeover, a natural disaster, industry collapse, unprecedented liability in a legal claim, etc.

The existing board can navigate these trying times, and its longevity and strong relationship with the CEO will be a benefit. However, the addition of one or two change agents to the board of a company in distress is a common scenario. These members often bring with them a discrete set of skills in turning companies around, or with solid contacts with professionals in the bankruptcy area. Now the company needs someone who understands how to operate under a debtors-in-possession framework, when to reorganize, when to liquidate, and what attorneys and accountants to bring in and assist.

Often the answer is a merger or sale of a division or of the company itself. Now contacts within the industry, with competitors, and with the right investment banker can open doors and shorten the lengthy process of identifying a buyer.

Perhaps the CEO will have to be replaced. The board must then become very involved and active, interviewing potential replacements, and even stepping in to fill the role of acting CEO until the company is stabilized and a solution is in place. The time commitments, additional meetings, teleconferences and difficult decisions can easily double or triple the workload a board member would have expected during a normal year.

> Unfortunately, boards are risk adverse...most of them don't need any more confrontation in their lives...so they are slow to act. It is hard for them to rid themselves of the fear and to take action to rid themselves of a non-performing CEO.
>
> Dennis Anderson, Chairman, ANDCOR

THE BAD BOARD MEMBER

Is a bad board member just the opposite of a good one? Well, not exactly. During our research, we would follow up our discussion of what characterized a good board member by asking the people we interviewed to contrast that with examples of bad directors they had observed.

CEOs would often chuckle at that and then describe instances where obstreperous directors had stood in their way, openly disrupted board meetings or tried to meddle in internal personnel or operational activities of the company where they did not belong. To most CEOs, bad directors were those who didn't understand the business or thwarted the direction the management team was taking. This is not surprising in that CEOs, almost by definition, are driving towards a target and feel tremendous pressure to achieve quarterly goals and get results. Their most common complaints were about directors that were too active, perceived as overstepping their bounds. CEOs also described directors who tried to micro-manage or undermine the CEOs authority by dealing directly with other executives.

Fellow directors saw things a bit differently. They complained about the inactive director. They described bad board members as not attending meetings regularly, missing or being late for teleconferences, dozing off, staring at their smart phone and texting during a meeting, or just not being prepared. Directors who take their responsibilities seriously resent those who do not.

Another common complaint was the unqualified director, also referred to as the golfing buddy director. This was noted again and again. The CEO feels under-supported or threatened by a strong group of directors and appoints a ringer, a friend, someone who will support his/her views and can be relied upon during the meeting for reassurance. Rarely is this individual qualified for the role, and, unfortunately, this is evident to everyone else in the room.

> It was clear from my first board meeting, I thought, "Who is this guy?" Turns out he was a long-term employee of the Chairman, a golfing buddy, and a crony. He never said much, made no contribution really. And he just wasn't smart enough to add anything to the discussion. I guess he just made the Chairman feel more comfortable, less threatened. It was a waste of a board seat if you ask me.
>
> Director of a NYSE company

Also mentioned was the director with an axe to grind. These individuals insisted on using the boardroom as a podium for describing their own problems with their businesses, airing their political views, or trying to force a solution or a supplier on a problem that the company didn't have or didn't want. These directors were viewed as self-centered and as wasting a lot of time.

Occasional examples of personality conflicts surfaced between the CEO and a board member or among members themselves. While rare, these were ugly and difficult to resolve.

SUMMARY

What makes a good board member? Possessing those two universal requirements— the ability to work well with the CEO and other members of the board, and financial acumen— and the right match of skill sets and experience for the challenges facing the company in its corporate life cycle.

To some, the role of director may sound easy. All you need to do is play well with others and understand financial statements, right? When things are going well in the company, it can be that simple and that enjoyable. But, as we pointed out in Chapter One, you need to balance the rewards of being a director with the potential risks. The demands on the director depend on the company's stage of development, the other directors' skills and abilities and the CEOs expectations and needs. In balancing the factors to reach your decision to join a board, recognize that risks can present the best opportunities to learn and season your business experiences.

5

WHAT DO YOU BRING TO THE TABLE?

Never sell yourself short. I was a nurse, an associate provost, and federal administrator with a serious hearing loss in my right ear. After I was on several boards, one of the CEOs commented that my caring concern about educational funding for America's future, my intensity when listening and my political optimism were my strengths. Everyone else would have considered them handicaps.

Carolyne K. Davis, (former) board member of
seven publicly traded companies

Picture this: the CEO of a well-known company in your area is at lunch with a member of his board. They are discussing the need to fill a seat left open by the resignation of a long-time member who is leaving to take on a new role for her company in Asia. Your name comes up. The CEO shakes his head and says, "I don't know that name. Who do they work for?" You fill in the blanks. What would they say? How would someone describe you today? What stands out? What qualifications, accomplishments, and affiliations would they point to first? Sound impressive?

In this chapter we will profile three current directors, explore what qualifications made them successful candidates, and how they arrived at their first seat on a corporate board. (We have changed their names or cities, and some of the identifying details in each vignette, but the process described is factual and typical of the first-time director story.) In each profile the keys to becoming a director centered on a record of achievement, skills that matched the company's current needs, and visibility or personal relationships. A self-assessment tool is provided to assist you in seeing your current abilities and in identifying areas where additional experience or skills may be required.

FIRST SEAT: VENTURE-BACKED STARTUP

At the height of the Internet start-up frenzy, Don got a call about a board seat for a young company in Denver. Although he did not know the caller, a close mutual friend, a banker whose business judgment Don admired, had referred the company president to him. He flew in and met with the president and the chairman of the company and quickly decided it was not for him. He graciously declined to pursue the discussion, but offered a few ideas and left the door open. The company was sold a few months later, and the management team went on to found a new enterprise focusing on a middleware application for the financial services industry.

A year later, Don received a call from the chairman of this new enterprise. She wanted to discuss a seat on the board of the new business. Intrigued, Don sensed a better fit and perceived a management team that had matured from the sobering aftermath of the market crash. This time, he had an interest in actively pursuing the role of director.

The chairman was interested in Don because of his background as a CIO of a major player in the financial services industry. Although Don had been working as an independent investor for the past several years, he had kept up with his professional contacts and still did an occasional consulting project for his previous employer. His ability to evaluate product development, recruit technical talent, and open the doors for a beta test within a large client were crucial contributions to this young organization.

Don's earlier assignments had included the sale of a unique piece of technology, developed by the parent company, to a small group of investors in California. It turned out that one of these investors was now active in the venture fund that was considering backing the Denver firm with a second round of $14 million. Quickly, it all came together. Don met with the venture capital representatives who were comfortable with his candidacy. The chairman offered him a seat, the second round was funded, and Don began contributing in his new role as a director.

Don had no prior corporate board experience. What he did have was *relevant skills* specific to the core business of software development within the financial services industry. In addition to a *strong track record of achievement* in his previous position as CIO of a major company, he had a *prior relationship* with two of the primary influencers on the board—the Chairman and the venture capital representative. Don's demonstrated *financial acumen* and *a visible profile* in the industry sealed the deal.

FIRST SEAT: COMPANY PREPARING TO FILE INITIAL PUBLIC OFFERING (IPO)

Andrew began his career in sales. He moved through the ranks of several companies in the computer and technologies sector, eventually serving on the executive management team of a large private company in Boston. He was well known in the industry, often quoted in the trade press and a frequent panelist at conferences and trade shows. Three years ago, he took the role of president for a large public company in Atlanta. His previous exposure to the boardroom had been as an executive presenting to the board. Now, as president and a member of his company's board, he was adding the experience of assisting in the preparation for and management of the quarterly meetings, the principles of corporate governance, the protocol of boardroom behavior, and the reporting and filing processes required in a public company.

Last year Jerry, a long-time colleague, approached him about a board seat. Andrew and Jerry had begun their career in sales together, and met while attending training for their company fifteen years ago. Although they had left to work for competing businesses three years later, they had kept in touch and often met for a drink at industry gatherings. Jerry had started a successful business in distributing and repairing peripheral storage devices and was preparing his company for an initial public offering. His investment bankers had advised Jerry to assemble a board that had depth and expertise in the industry: some "marquee value" (meaning names that would be easily recognizable to industry analysts following the stocks of similar businesses), spotless records, and public company experience.

Jerry asked Andrew for some advice on assembling a new board. Because Andrew had been in his new role as president for almost three years, he felt he had the time to contribute and could learn a lot by participating in the IPO process with another organization. He knew he could help Jerry get up to speed with the corporate governance principles, and benefit from the systems he had put in place for reporting and pulling together the board packages each quarter. As it turned out, the two companies shared the same law firm, and the law partner on Andrew's account had also recommended Andrew to Jerry.

Andrew agreed to take on this first seat as an independent director on a soon-to-be public board. He had prior corporate board experience as an insider, as the president of his company. He also had *relevant skills* specific to the core business of technology distribution, sales and corporate governance. He had a *strong track record of achievement* in his current role. Andrew had a *prior relationship* with two of the primary influencers—the founder and his attorney. Demonstrated *financial acumen* and *a visible profile* in the industry and with the analyst community completed the picture.

FIRST SEAT: DIRECTOR ON A LARGE PUBLIC COMPANY BOARD

Sandy's case is unusual in two respects: her first seat was on the board of a large, publicly held company and she is an academic. However, she still followed a pattern similar to the cases we have already explored.

Sandy is a full professor at a prestigious university in Southern California. She often teaches in an executive seminar series designed to keep CEOs up to date with the latest in supply chain management theory and practice. As part of her research, companies agree to participate in yearlong studies with teams of her graduate students. The results are often published or become part of case studies that she uses in her classes or presents to conferences.

One such intriguing case study led Sandy to a discussion about a board seat with a public company in Texas. The business was growing rapidly and management was aggressively pursuing the latest in supply chain practices in order to cut costs and create a competitive advantage. Sandy was fascinated by the company and flattered by the offer, but declined. She felt her schedule was overloaded, she was in the middle of a multi-year commitment as departmental chair, and she was wary of adding to the stacks of reading already on her desk.

The CEO continued to pursue her. Finally, they agreed to a small consulting project that would occur during the summer and allow Sandy to get to know the company and the management team. She continued to consult for three more years. Her relationship with the CEO and several of the executives deepened. When her tenure as department chair ended, she had more control over her schedule and more free time. When the CEO again proposed the idea of taking a seat on the board, she accepted. At the same time, she ended her role as a consultant to the company.

Sandy had no prior corporate board experience. What she did have was *relevant skills* specific to the core business of manufacturing and supply chain management. She had a *strong track record of achievement* in academia, with the credentials of a full professor, department chair and a strong record of published research and case study. She had developed *a relationship* with several of the primary influencers on the board. Demonstrated *financial acumen* and *a visible profile* in the supply chain practice community rounded out her qualifications.

SELF-ASSESSMENT: DEVELOPING A CLEAR PICTURE OF YOUR QUALIFICATIONS FOR THE BOARD

By now, the picture is pretty clear. Although each individual we interviewed had a unique story about taking their first seat on a corporate board, four factors were common to all:

- Relevant skills specific to the core business

- Strong record of achievement

- Relationship with one or more influencers on the board

- Demonstrated financial acumen, social skills, and a visible profile

Let's take a look at how your own story would compare. We have developed this grid to assist executives in viewing their own background and experiences through the lens of the board selection process. Most readers will quickly note several areas of strength along with a gap or two. This information is useful for evaluating future opportunities and assignments. It allows you to make an on-purpose decision to fill in whatever blanks may exist for you—to obtain additional financial responsibilities, broaden your base of personal contacts in the community, or increase your visibility within trade association groups or among investors and analysts, etc. So open up your I-pad or grab a pen and paper and answer the following questions:

• RELEVANT SKILLS SPECIFIC TO THE CORE BUSINESS

This is the easiest place to start for most candidates. A look at your own resume should quickly yield three or four specific skill sets, an industry or market sector, and the companies at which you have made your mark. Don't confuse this with job titles. What you were called may or may not describe accurately what you know. The real question to ask yourself is: What have I mastered? What do I know how to do?

For example, are you skilled in the area of corporate finance? Then you are familiar with how to refinance debt, how to factor

accounts receivable, raise capital in the secondary markets or nego-
tiate a bridge loan. You have a definable, replicable skill. Common
areas of skill that are desirable in the board room include management, finance, information systems, marketing, and sales, just to
name a few. The narrower disciplines of law or accounting are also
important, but realize that the board will already have access to its
own corporate counsel and auditors.

Take a look at the depth or breadth of your skill set. If your area
is marketing, have you held marketing positions across a variety
of industries (like food, toys and real estate) or specifically within
one sector (such as consumer packaged goods or wholesale distribution)? Develop your own elevator speech and listen to it. As you
hear yourself described, summarized in just a few sentences, how
does it sound?

• STRONG RECORD OF ACHIEVEMENT

Now, shift gears. Instead of looking at what you know how to do
(your skill set) look at the proof that you have done it well. What
results can you point to? You should be able to easily describe three
or four instances where you have personally delivered or led a team
that accomplished some impressive results.

If you are not the CEO of a publicly traded company, then the
question is: what achievements can you bring to the boardroom that will get the board's attention? Certain arenas, like
public policy, research and government service, all offer opportunities. But the key to any opportunity, and to your next job,
is doing the current job so exceptionally well that everyone
notices.

Shirley Jackson, President of Rennsaeler Polytechnic Institute
and board member.

If your background is in corporate finance, for example, have
you successfully completed a major secondary offering during a
very difficult time in the market? This would demonstrate your
skill, and the high regard that the financial community holds you

in, with the result being a large capital infusion for your current employer. That's a strong, verifiable achievement.

The skilled marketer can point to the successful launch of a product line last year, the advertising campaign and distribution strategy she designed and the increase in sales since she took on the role of CMO. These are measurable, public results and they build a strong track record of performance and experience to draw from.

Here, titles do matter. It does help if your accomplishments are rewarded with a steady progression up the corporate ladder. Most directors have held the title of CEO or president at some point in their career. Of course, the role of president at Hewlett Packard means a lot more than the title of president in your own business or for a small manufacturing group. Many directors are in a senior executive role at a large corporation and do not have the title of CEO. Others are successful entrepreneurs, founders, or wealthy investors with no titles at all. Increasingly, boards are reaching out for technology and marketing backgrounds, bringing on people who have been a CTO or CIO, a CMO, or lead a foreign subsidiary. Most directors will be able to point to steadily increasing roles and responsibilities and the titles that go with them. If you are not a CEO yet, you should be headed in that direction.

- ## RELATIONSHIP WITH ONE OR MORE INFLUENCERS ON THE BOARD

This is where most candidates start to perceive a gap. Do you have established relationships with individuals who are in a position of influence with the board? Which board? Any board.

> It's about calibration. A wise candidate looks at the other directors currently on that board and calibrates his or her own background, experiences and skills against that group. Am I a likely fit? Realistically, few are qualified to serve on the board of a GE or Apple.
>
> George Fleck, Founder, G. Fleck/Board Services.

This is a test of the strength and breadth of your professional network. Over the course of your career, have you created and maintained contacts with people who are now serving as CEOs, presidents, advisors, directors or investors? If not, you may just be too young. It takes an arc of twenty to thirty years for the individuals you have entered the work force with to begin to emerge as powerful leaders in their own right.

On the other hand, if you can name many of these people as your colleagues, you may be in line for your first seat on a corporate board.

- ## Demonstrated financial acumen, social skills, and a visible profile

The concept of financial acumen has been explored in Chapter Four, but it's worth mentioning here again. A lack of financial understanding can only hold you back. If you possess it, and nothing else, it will probably not be enough to get you onto a board. The corporate world is full of analytics and bean counters and they don't become directors. But if you don't have it, even though you have many other strengths, it can keep you off the short list of candidates.

Let's take the example of marketing skill. If you are a creative genius and have the bright ideas behind all the best campaigns for your company's product, you may have made a real name for yourself in the industry. If you are known for leaving all the details to someone else, and making a big splash while also running over budget, you won't add much to the boardroom discussions on cash flow or the earnings outlook for the quarter. The same holds true of visionaries in the technology arena, or inventors, founders and entrepreneurs. Human resource professionals, lawyers, academicians, scientists, and researchers—all may have outstanding credentials or accomplishments in their field. They may or may not have sufficient financial acumen to take a seat on a corporate board. They may be just the right individuals to serve on an advisory board or in a paid consulting capacity to the organization, however.

Why me? Well, I think I am a desirable candidate because I have been the Chairman and CEO of a large, multi-state bank and the CEO of an interstate community banking organization, as well. Banking is the perfect background, I think. It cuts across all industries, all types of business. No matter what your company does, it needs a bank. So, after twenty plus years, I've pretty much seen it all. And I know a lot of people in this town. I can get quite a lot done just by picking up the phone, and that can make a difference for a new company or management team. A strong board can really make a difference.

Former CEO, banking executive and board member

• Social skills, executive presence and visibility

Social skills, also known as executive presence, are code words for all those intangible attributes a candidate carries into the boardroom. These cannot be ascertained from a resume: the ability to work harmoniously and effectively with other directors and management, a reputation for honesty, integrity and fairness, discretion, and social graces. This is why personal referrals to the chairman, or referral through another board member, are the way most candidates become board members. It means they have been "vetted" and found to be appropriate.

All board members, but especially the CEO, are looking for a new director who will be socially reliable. They want someone who has a sense of humor, clarity in his or her communications… in other words, someone who is not stupid.

Constance Horner, served on several Fortune 100 boards, including Pfizer as lead director, and as governance chair on three other boards.

What, exactly, does this all mean? Well, if you are a successful fast-track executive or professional and are currently enjoying a steady rise through the ranks of your corporation, you probably have executive presence. Let's try to put it into words. It's the ability to socialize gracefully with individuals of many different backgrounds in many different situations. Whether you are on a golf course, at an expensive restaurant for a business dinner, or on the podium at a sales meeting, you are able to conduct yourself appropriately and put others at ease. You can present complex ideas, effectively and articulately, in front of small or large groups, without undue nervousness or discomfort. Others would describe you as knowing just what to do or always saying the right thing. You are not known for making gaffes, derogatory comments or inappropriate jokes or remarks that offend others. Your behavior at an office party or in a bar with business associates does not make the office grapevine. In short, you are what is called "socially reliable."

• VISIBILITY

Which leaves just one other area left in the self-assessment: personal visibility. If you are a highly qualified candidate with the desire to serve on a corporate board, yet no one has ever heard of you outside of the confines of your own corporation, then you may as well be invisible. We will discuss the practice of maintaining a reasonable profile, within those communities that are meaningful to you, and why it is an essential part of your career plan in Chapter Eight. For now, you should complete your self-assessment by asking yourself this question, "If a CEO or a search firm was looking to find three to five high profile, successful individuals in my sector or industry, would my name be on that list? How?"

> When I looked at putting that board together, I was looking for five different people, really. I had in mind a technologist, someone that really knew sales, a finance guy, a solid marketer, and then a generalist—you know, someone who had really been around the block and knew this business, how it makes money and what can go wrong. And I found it. Took me awhile, but good directors are out there, you just have to put the word out and be willing to take the time to make the calls and put it together.
>
> Paul Thomas, former chairman, Artisoft Technologies

SUMMARY

Is your name Colin Powell? Carly Fiorina or Jack Welch? What about Bill Gates, Sheryl Sandberg or Larry Page? If you are not a celebrity, a famous politician, a diplomat or a Wall Street icon, then you will need something else. You will need the six qualifications that are common to almost every director as they take their first seat on a corporate board: a relevant skill set, a strong record of personal achievement, a prior relationship or personal referral, financial acumen, social skills, and a visible profile in the industry or within your geographic community.

6

READY OR NOT? TIMING AND POSITIONING ALONG YOUR CAREER PATH

Now it gets personal. You already know what a corporation expects from its board members. You have evaluated what skills and qualifications you possess. You may even be aware of an open seat at a company that could really use what you have to offer, but is this the right time for you?

An executive search firm survey indicates board members may well spend an average of one hundred seventy-three hours annually on board matters, including review and preparation, meeting attendance and travel. That's more than four forty-hour weeks. The board of the average Fortune 1000 company meets eight times a year.

The time commitment undoubtedly differs depending on the size of the company, the stage of its development (startups can take inordinate amounts of time, as can acquisitions, cut backs, and bankruptcy). Smaller companies, located nearby, may meet in a formal board meeting only four times a year (the range is three to eighteen times a year) and your travel may be a short trip down the hall.

How much time does it really take? Well, the classic answer is 'that depends.' I have been in the boardroom of large public companies and small, venture-backed start-ups. They are two different worlds.

If you are sitting on the board of a public company, you are usually dealing with an organization that has maturity and scale. They have infrastructure in place that surrounds and supports each of their core business processes. You are acting in a fiduciary capacity for the shareholders. You can confidently review summary financial statement info, and have a strategic dialogue. You can offer advice on complicated transactions, etc.

However, none of this applies when you are dealing with small, pre-public companies. As the representative of a large venture fund, I could take nothing for granted. You have to dig deeply into the financial statements. You cannot assume anything. Often, an inexperienced CEO is trying to manage a large cash infusion in a high growth environment without established processes or delegated functions. The management team has to prove the reliability of their systems and financial statements to the board before you can move on to advise or govern.

These young businesses can make extraordinary demands on their director's time. You must set some realistic expectations and boundaries up front.

Anthony Ibargüen, CEO of Quench, Inc., Director of Insight
Enterprises, Inc. and (former) President of Tech Data Corporation

You need to add time for the attendance at committee meetings— and usually a board member serves on one or two committees that meet, on average, three times a year. The good news is that most committee meetings are generally short and held immediately before or after the board meeting. Sometimes they are conducted in teleconferences, so there is not additional travel time for committee meetings.

This is not a game for the faint-hearted or for those already short of time. In order to do a good job as a director, you must devote the necessary time. Efforts to cover your tail with broad stroke questions will only take you so far. And remember, you not only have the CEO and the senior management to impress, the other directors are usually very astute at identifying the good directors from the impostor.

> Think carefully about time zone issues for your travel and for calls back to your own business or home, as well as conference-call times. It may sound wonderful to head to NYC from the West Coast six times a year for board meetings. But unless you can do additional business, or fulfill personal obligations (e.g., your parents still live in the Bronx) while making the trip, those five hour flights can get very old, very fast.
>
> West Coast CEO and Chairman

You must (we repeat must) make time to not only attend the board meetings, but also prepare for the meetings. That means you have to have some semblance of control over your life. If there is a personal crises looming, a new baby to love, a teenager who is perfecting her tennis game and is a likely candidate for a full scholarship, a parent who is recently widowed and needing some extra time...then you need to evaluate whether you really have control over your life at this time.

If you are constantly reacting to a demanding boss who believes the only reason you exist on earth is to respond to his demands, then you are already in jeopardy. To think that a board meeting will be an acceptable excuse to avoid an important client meeting, or miss a deadline, is a serious mistake. Either get the boss to agree that this outside board seat is in the best interests of the company and will be a priority so that when you are scheduled to be at a meeting you will be there—or forget it. Nothing taints your reputation faster than missing meetings. The unwritten message to the other board members, who probably have equally, if not more, important projects at their own office, is that you are more important than they are. No one likes that message.

Another major search firm tells their candidates that a board seat takes up to nineteen days a year, roughly a day and a half a month. If trouble begins to brew—or acquisitions or mergers get put on the table—you can double that time commitment. It is hard to get off a public board, especially when the downward slide has begun, and there is really no such thing as a gracious exit. Particularly in tough times, other members will see you as a traitor, the press will be all over you, and the plaintiff's lawyers still have your name on the list. Furthermore, you will suffer the guilt of abandoning the team mid-stream.

A thoughtful answer to the question of whether you are ready or not requires you to take an honest look at three arenas: your personal/family life, your financial position, and your professional life. Just to keep you sharp, we'll start each section off with a trick question.

PERSONAL/FAMILY LIFE

Q. When is the right time to take your first seat on a corporate board?

A. When your personal and family life is stable and predictable, and can flex with the unforeseen demands on your time as a new board member.

Trick question? Of course. By their very nature, families and personal lives are full of their own unforeseen demands and crisis. Heart attacks and car accidents, aging parents and unruly teenagers, weddings and divorces—the stuff of life certainly doesn't take a back seat to serving on a board. Nor should it. But there is such a thing as common sense.

Accepting a seat usually marks the beginning of a five to ten year commitment. Although some positions are more short term in nature, such as accepting an assignment to evaluate the sale of a company or oversee a bankruptcy, or act as an interim chair until the next CEO is found, most board seats call for a lengthy relationship. Several of the directors we interviewed had been on a board for twenty years, many for over ten years, and most for more than five.

Before making that type of commitment, you should be reasonably free of large, known disruptions in your personal life that might render you unable to attend meetings or prepare adequately. Use common sense. If you are expecting twins, your father was just diagnosed with Alzheimer's or you are in the midst of a difficult divorce—wait a few years before pursuing the role of director. You'll be glad you did.

FINANCIAL POSITION

Q. When is the right time to take on your first seat on a corporate board?

A. When you are financially stable, have achieved (your own definition of) personal wealth, and do not need the fees or stock options offered to corporate directors.

Trick question? Of course! Given the recent severe recession, no one may ever feel financially stable. If you are motivated by money (and most people in business are), then you may never feel you have accomplished all your goals in the area of personal wealth. Director's fees are usually adequate, but stock options can be significant. Wouldn't everyone like to have been the initial directors on the board of Goggle? Or Apple? Or Amazon? No matter what may have happened to those stocks in the years that followed, their initial public offerings made a lot of directors very wealthy, indeed.

Without minimizing the potential upside of becoming a director, you have to be prepared for the possibility that there will be no upside. Ideally, the position you are considering is interesting to you without regard to the possible personal financial outcomes. This is a key point, because of your primary fiduciary responsibility to the shareholders of the corporation. Not to yourself.

If your own personal fortunes took a turn for the worse, you do not want to be in a position that could influence your judgment as a director. If you were strapped for cash and the sale of the company would allow you to raise much needed funds, could you put that aside when considering a potential offer for acquisition? If, as a show of good faith in the company's future, all directors are required to own shares, or expected to buy additional shares when the market is down, or not to sell their shares when the market is weak—are you prepared for that?

Directors are insiders. They have to abide by very strict rules concerning when they can or cannot sell stock in the company. This may mean sitting on the sidelines during windows of opportunity when the stock could be bought at what appeared at the time to be a bargain price or sold at a hefty profit. If you want to make your money trading stocks, don't sit on a board.

During the heyday of the Internet frenzy, I sat on the board of a small company in the technology sector. After a somewhat innocuous press release announcing a new deal with a large, recognizable client, our stock soared. Suddenly, stock I had purchased for less than $10/share was selling for over $50/share. Wow. My spouse was going nuts. Sell! Sell! All he could think of was cashing in and getting out with our windfall.

Of course, that was not possible. Not only was the company in a quiet period where trading was forbidden by the SEC, but directors were in possession of material information about the company's plans for the future and the financial results for the quarter, none of which had yet been made public. Also, it would have just plain looked bad for the company if suddenly all the insiders had bailed out on the stock. So, I did what I had to do, which was nothing. Hold.

The market cooled, the bubble burst, and our windfall blew away. My spouse brings that up at least once a year. If you want to make money trading stocks, don't think you're going to do it from your seat on a board.

Director, publicly-held technology company in the Northwest

PROFESSIONAL LIFE

Q. When is the right time to take your first seat on a corporate board?

A. When you have all the answers, have already made your mark in life, have nothing left to prove, and plenty of patience and time on your hands.

Trick question? Now you're catching on! If you even think you know all the answers, you would make an insufferable board member. However, if you are confident of your skills and have a broad perspective on business, perhaps you are at that magical point in your career where you are starting to ask some good questions. Now, that counts for something.

If you have an impressive track record as a results-oriented CEO, executive, professional or academic, then you must have a somewhat aggressive personality and a strong desire to win. Admit it; that's what has gotten you so far along in business. However, left unchecked, this competitive streak can be destructive in the boardroom. Ideally, you have achieved enough individually that you have gotten over yourself, and can sincerely support the success and growth of the CEO and senior management of another company. You no longer feel you have to be the star, the center of attention at every meeting, the quarterback with the winning strategy. Or at least, not while you are in the boardroom.

You have to remember that your job as a board member is to pick the coach, define the plays, and then stay off the field. You should not be managing the managers. And you sure aren't the quarterback, so stay the hell out of operations....If you think being on the board means being a bigger boss, you're wrong. If you're going to be effective as a board member, you have to have gotten over your own ego.

Jock Patton, director, Hypercom

There are two other times in your career that we want to mention: the dropping-out stage and the pre-retirement stage. It is probably best to make your full court press for a board seat before you announce your plans to take several years off for personal reasons or your plans for an early retirement. Most board members, and especially CEOs who are still working fifty-five hours a week, are a little uncomfortable with someone who clearly has achieved some life balance. While that is what all of us claim to strive for, those that haven't arrived get a little nervous around, and suspicious of, those who have made the decision.

The second concern is that the 'not working full-time' or early retirement status somehow implies you are no longer engaged. While not necessarily true, it is a common perception out there.

Our best advice is to hang on until you have your first board seat. Don't make the change from full-time work status until you have the chair. From that platform, you can then perform so well as a board member you will be invited to sit on another board — because you now have the extra time!

If you are currently acting as the CEO of your own company, you have a place to vent your ego. CEOs, and other successful executives, like the opportunity of running the show, but when you are in the boardroom of another company, you need to take a more passive role, learning new strategies, advising other CEOs, mentoring other members of management.

Can you see the difference? Here's a little test for you. Quick, name three directors on the board of Google. Okay, then name at least two on the board of Apple. Drawing a blank? Bet you can name their CEOs—Mark Zuckerberg and Tim Cook, right? The point is, serving on the board is a behind-the-scenes role. No one knows your name, nor should they. You give no press interviews, you are not pictured in *Fortune* magazine, no one attributes the success of the company to your brilliant strategies or maneuverings around the boardroom table. You are not the star. You are not the CEO. There is a difference. And, for many people, the ability to finesse this new role as a board member does not come naturally until they are of a certain age.

Age usually drives experience. You should have seen both a boom and a bust, the good times and the bad. Your frame of reference can't be just the recent Internet boom, or the prolonged cycle of expansion we had in housing and construction. You need someone that remembers what the letters RTC stand for.

John Lewis, Chairman of the Board, Blood Systems, Inc.; (former) President of Sun Community Bancorp.

It's time to address this issue of age and seasoning. Seasoning is often a euphemism for age. Younger executives, flush with their first big success, often feel ready to take on the world. It appears to them that they have won, and are now ready to show everyone else how easy this whole game is. That attitude comes from a lack of seasoning. Until you have steered a company through economic downturns, reversals, and full-blown recessions, you don't really know what the second half of the game is about.

Business has cycles, the economy has cycles, and human leadership has its cycles, too. Success and winning is just round one. Next comes failure, trying times, and personal growth. Most people just gain experience but, for those willing to go the distance, the outcome can be wisdom. When corporations are serious about a functional, active board, they recruit seasoned executives with broad-based experiences that can add real value and leadership in the good times and the bad times ahead.

SUMMARY

The trouble with awareness, good business judgment, and experience is that it takes a lifetime to get it.

Alan P. Hald, Partner, American Legal Funding, LLC.;
(former) Chairman of the Board, iCrossing

Most of the directors we spoke with were between forty-five and sixty-five years of age. Over half were not currently acting as the CEO of another organization, although most had been in the role of CEO or had significant responsibilities in government, academia or a non-profit at some point in their career. When asked, most responded that a candidate under forty years old would be unusual, though not unheard of. It's difficult to have twenty-five years of solid experience under your belt and only be thirty-seven years old, but there are no hard and fast rules.

Timing is everything. When the thought of serving on a corporate board first emerges, an individual is often too early in his or her career to be a viable candidate. Setting the goal helps bring into focus what is missing, and allows a strategic approach to building the requisite skill set. The act of building these skills is then synonymous with becoming a successful executive. Almost by definition, once you have the ability to be a director, you do not have the time!

So here's the answer to that trick question, "When is the right time to take your first seat on a corporate board?" When you are at that point in your life where you are too busy for people that waste your time, but can always find time for the people you love or admire; when you realize that the money you have is enough for the life you want; and you are at a place in your career where you have a lot to offer, but still want to learn. Then, you're as ready as you'll ever be. When the right seat comes up, take it.

PART III
THE OPEN SEAT:
WILL YOU BE IN THE
RIGHT PLACE AT THE
RIGHT TIME?

By now you know if you have what it takes— the skills and experience to contribute at the board level, and if this is the right time in your career to take on a significant new role.

Still in the running? Then, let's get down to the business of matching your preparation with an opportunity. In the next chapter, we'll explain the board member selection process and how more than eight thousand directors are seated every year. You'll learn about the role that executive search firms can play, and how to get your name on the short list. In fact, you'll be taking a simple test to determine your Individual Short List Quotient, and the results may surprise you.

We'll walk you through the offer process and show you how to be sure that you're making a match that is right for you. You'll learn what is negotiable, and what is not, and how the process differs from accepting a job offer.

Finally, current directors and CEOs will share some last words of advice with you on how to become part of the team, gracefully, when you take that first seat on a corporate board.

7

THE BOARD MEMBER SELECTION PROCESS

How often does a board need to select a new member? What causes a seat to become vacant or a new one to be added? How does a board go about determining who will be their newest member?

Well, first let's do the math. We'll use some round numbers here to get us in the ballpark. The last time we checked, there were almost two thousand companies listed on the New York Stock Exchange, over three thousand companies trading on the NASDAQ and about six hundred companies listed on the American Stock Exchange. There are approximately fifty thousand seats held by directors of publicly traded companies, many of whom serve on more than one board and most of whom serve for an average of eight years. The average number of directors is 9.2 according to a recent study at the Corporate Library. What's missing is an accurate count of the seats held by independent directors on the boards of privately held U.S. corporations, joint ventures, and pre-IPO businesses backed by venture capital. Many of these are just as large and sophisticated as your average public company. We think a very conservative estimate here would be fifteen to twenty thousand private board seats. This would put the universe of seats for directors of public and large privately held corporations in the U.S. at well over seventy thousand.

Trading Company	Number of director seats	Total
New York Stock Exchange	18,400	
NASDAQ	27,600	46,000
American Stock Exchange	5,400	51,400
Private Companies	15,000—20,000 (estimate)	70,000

Using an average tenure of eight years, logic tells you that at least eight to nine thousand board seats need to be filled in any given year. For a mature organization with a nine to twelve member board, that's about one vacancy a year. For a relatively new company that just seated a five or six member board when it went public two years ago, there may be no vacancies for several years.

WHAT CAUSES A SEAT TO BECOME VACANT OR A NEW ONE TO BE ADDED

Normally, a board starts looking for a new member when a vacancy is caused by mandatory retirement, death or disability or a voluntary resignation. Another reason boards go looking is to add a particular skill set or specific expertise. A company that has recently purchased another line of business may need additional knowledge about that industry—or research and development information—or new contacts in a different arena.

Less often, new members are added because the CEO (or another board member) identifies someone who is so spectacular, with so much to offer the company, that they are afraid to wait for a vacancy to occur. To be sure the person doesn't sign on with a competitor, or take on too other many boards, an individual is sometimes invited to join even when there isn't a vacancy. We've seen this happen with government officials, for instance, who are about to leave government and make themselves available to the private sector. Usually the board has only to adopt a simple resolution to increase the number of directors on the board.

HOW DOES THE BOARD GO ABOUT SELECTING THEIR NEWEST MEMBER?

Although many companies see what they do as a unique or individual process, our interviews revealed it to be many variations on just one theme—commonly referred to as *the grid*. We'll take a look at how three boards have used this grid process—one illustrates the formal approach of a Fortune 500 organization; the other two are smaller companies, one working closely with a search firm and the other relying on personal contacts. We'll also check in with some of the national search firms that have established practices to facilitate the board member selection process, and discover what trends are creating opportunities for today's newest directors.

THE FORTUNE 500 PROCESS

Large public companies, blessed with corporate secretaries and support staff that provide liaison work for the CEO and the Board of Directors, have the advantage of sophisticated resources to help in the recruitment of additional board members.

The search for new directors is conducted through formally constructed governance, nomination or board affairs committees. Through the adoption of formal operating principles, first placed in vogue by General Motors in the late 1980s, these companies outline recruitment criteria and have them formally adopted by the full board of directors.

These general principles are reflected in the development of the grid or table. Across the top will be a listing of the areas in which the board has determined the need for expertise. Down the left hand column, each current director would be listed. Checkmarks are made horizontally across the grid to denote what areas of expertise or skills are provided by that director to the board. Many directors will overlap or others provide multiple skill sets. The blanks that remain are indicative of what that board needs to look for when recruiting its next member. The boxes will change over time as the company encounters new challenges or enters foreign markets or divests itself of a certain line of business. If age is a factor, then the grid may also include a column noting when directors will be retiring and their expertise will need to be replaced. A sample grid might look like this:

Public Company XYZ Board of Directors

Director	Retirement Date	Financial Acumen	Industry Knowledge	Regulatory Experience	Technology Expertise	Marketing Skills	Research & Development	Qualified for Audit Comm.?
A	2019	X	X	X				X
B	2017	X			X			X
C	2025	X	X					
D	2025	X	X				X	
E	2018	X	X					X
New								

Once the company identifies a specific need, or realizes that certain current expertise will be retiring soon, the company develops a description of the skill and knowledge set they are seeking. In our sample grid above, the company will be looking for a new director with a strong marketing skill set.

In addition to the expertise they are looking for, Fortune 500 companies often have written guidelines for the *type of individuals* they want to attract. What follows is an excerpt from such an organization's broad framework for director recruitment:

RECRUITING CRITERIA

Some basic considerations to use as criteria for adding a Board member:

- The candidate must have an outstanding reputation and be associated with a first class institution; he/she must be nationally recognized in a particular area of expertise;

- The candidate cannot serve on the board of another [similar] company, competitor, or other company where the resulting interlock would violate Section 8 of the Clayton Act;

- The candidate should not be associated with an institution, which would pose an existing or potential conflict of interest;

- The candidate should not represent a special interest which would inhibit the candidate's broad perspective of our enterprise; and

- The candidate must be willing to devote the necessary preparation time and be available for at least [the full] Board meetings currently required in our schedule.

- Naturally, there are other considerations when adding future Board members. As we look ahead, we need to consider where [the Company] is headed and ensure that our Board is adequately represented in the areas of: Retail Strategy; Consumer Marketing; Communication and Information Services; Technology; Healthcare and Financial Services

- In addition to outstanding expertise in these emerging growth areas, consideration should be given to the following criteria; Minority Representation; Female Representation; and Geographic Diversity

- Finally, we need to consider the age of potential candidates to avoid clusters of retirement and to maximize continuity of Board membership.

With the results of the grid process and recruiting criteria in mind, the full board is then appraised of the need for a new director. They are asked to provide suitable names to the CEO or governance committee chair. Often, this step is all that is needed to surface eight to ten outstanding candidates for consideration. These names are referred to as the short list. No notice is ever posted of a vacancy. You will not find open board seats on the Internet or in the newspaper. Boards will announce when they have seated a new member, they will not announce that they are searching for one. The only way to become a part of the selection process is by having your name on the short list.

WHEN A SEARCH FIRM COMES INTO PLAY

Many CEOs we interviewed felt very strongly that the use of a reputable search firm greatly enhanced their selection process. Others were quite vocal in their opposition, one going so far as to say that "search firms are only for people that don't have any friends"—meaning those CEOs without an established professional network of their own.

Our research found that most boards have used search firms on occasion. The reasons most often cited were:

- Looking for a candidate in a new line of business where we do not have established contacts

- Looking for a candidate from a foreign country in which we are setting up operations

- Looking for a candidate with experience in a specific technology we will be implementing

- Looking for candidates qualified for service on our audit committee

- Looking for female or minority candidates

- Wanting to assure that the best possible list of candidates is in front of us —we only know who we know, show us who else is out there

Among the national firms most often mentioned were Spencer Stuart, Korn/Ferry, and Heidrick&Struggles. There was also mention of several exceptional, smaller firms who specialize in certain industry sectors or certain regions of the country—Board Services in the Northeast or True in Silicon Valley, for example.

A search firm will provide the board with a long list of possible candidates. We've heard of lists as large as thirty, but usually they are a more manageable number of ten to fifteen. The search firm's presentation includes the candidates' resume (or an extracted version to standardize the review process), references from people who have worked with the candidate, and comments from the search firm about the individual's performance. These comments are synthesized from former bosses and co-workers, general reputation in the industry, and any other sources deemed relevant. The search firms all seek to provide similar, comparable information on each individual for ease of review.

At this point, the process becomes the same whether a search firm has been used or all the names have been generated internally. The list is carefully reviewed by the Chairman of the Board, the CEO, and if applicable, by the members of the committee responsible for board development or governance. The serious work then begins of culling through the connections the company and current board members may have with the individuals who surfaced as the most likely candidates. The list is usually cut back to three or four candidates for the interview. Some companies may rely on the governance committee chair and the CEO to do the interviewing; others include a connecting director (someone who either knows the candidate or knows someone who knows the candidate). A few companies may include the entire governance committee membership in the interview.

It is at this point that considerations of fit come into play. How will the candidate relate to the other board members? Is the candidate socially reliable? What contributions will the candidate make to this company, and to this board of directors?

From these interviews a consensus will emerge as to who would be the ideal candidate to recommend to the full board. In the best-run companies, that candidate will then be given the opportunity to meet with the other board members, and, perhaps, some members of senior management, particularly in the area of expertise relevant to the candidate's experience.

Finally, the candidate will then be introduced to the board, and a vote taken to invite them to serve. Most companies can add members at any time, but if they have sound governance practices, the new member will be invited to stand for shareholder election at the next annual meeting and then be formally elected to serve. Timing can get tricky, especially in the circumstances where a company does not want a candidate to get away. In that case, the candidate can be asked to join immediately, and then elected at the next annual meeting. We know of no case where shareholders have ever objected to the timing issues—or rejected a candidate who is already serving as the result of an election by the board.

Mid-cap company search targets member with expertise in deregulation

A mid-size energy company knew it had to enhance its expertise in the area of de-regulation. Clearly, this would be the central challenge facing the business in the coming years. No sense in re-inventing the wheel, they wisely concluded. What had already worked in other industries, and what didn't work well?

In these discussions at the governance committee level, the committee members went through the industries that had been deregulated and decided that the airlines and telecommunications industries must have valuable lessons to be learned. Discussing the issue before the full board, one board member identified an individual who had an outstanding reputation in a deregulated industry; had worked many years earlier with another board member on a state agency; and had positioned themselves well in a leading company through a series of promotions and additional assignments.

Knowledge of the person's work history, contributions to government, and apparent success at the current company led the governance committee to go looking more closely at the candidate. Board members who had personal information, or knew people who knew the candidate's current employer and colleagues, offered to do some discreet gathering of personal information.

The feedback was all positive— and within months the candidate had been approached, courted, and signed on as a new board member.

SMALLER COMPANIES MAY USE A LESS FORMAL VERSION OF THE GRID PROCESS

Your first seat on a corporate board is more likely to be with a smaller public company or one that is privately held. These organizations rarely have the formal committee structures seen in the Fortune 500. Formal board nomination or development committees are unusual. Instead, the CEO and one or two close advisors will huddle to discuss the needs of the business and what the current board may be missing. Though often verbal, the thought process (and the results) will be very similar to that documented by the grid.

When we interviewed the CEO of a small, specialty pharmaceutical company he had just completed a board selection process that had expanded his four-member board to six.

He spent over forty percent of his time for four months overseeing the process. He was determined to find the right individuals who could move the company from a research and development laboratory to a drug producing entity with potential profits. He and one other member of the board spent hours defining exactly what the company's needs would be over the next few years and what kind of individual could help get them there. They specifically identified the following needs:

- **Technology** Someone who was distinguished in the relevant academic niche, but who also had the respect of the industry and who represented cutting edge thinking, experience in current research efforts, and a broad perspective about what opportunities were ahead for the industry.

- **Solid Financial Expertise** Someone who had experience in the industry, but not a competitor. They hoped for some prior CFO experience with a company that had undergone successful rapid growth.

- **Venture Capital Connections** Not necessarily someone who would invest in the company, but someone who was knowledgeable about financing options and capital strategies, and who had access and connections to the primary venture funds for this type of company.

In one of the new board members, the company was also hoping for an individual who knew the sales and marketing nuances of pharmaceuticals, and had managed dramatic growth in a company. They engaged a search firm founded by individuals who had previously served in the pharmaceutical and retail industries.

After receiving a detailed written description of what the company criteria was for the new board members, the search firm came back with twenty names for review. The CEO and one other board member studied the documentation, including resumes, referrals and search firm notes. Some resumes were immediately dismissed as not fitting the criteria. For instance, one individual had been in the industry, but his expertise was mostly in human resources, not a pressing need for the lab now. Three individuals withdrew their names. Of the remaining candidates, the CEO and the board member selected four candidates for interviews.

During the interview process, the emphasis shifted away from credentials and experience, to personality. Was the person friendly and open? Did the person have strong communication skills? Could the person elaborate on the resume? How would the person fit in with the other board members and management? How could the person contribute significantly to the company in the areas identified in the written criteria?

The CEO reported that all four interviews went well and any of the four could have made contributions to the company. One candidate turned out to be much stronger than the resume suggested and, "just blew us away with his knowledge and ideas".

But, the decision came down to two: one, a highly regarded academician/entrepreneur who had presented numerous papers at academic and industry meetings, had organized a national conference on topics directly relevant to the company, and had achieved high respect from other companies (as evidenced by consulting activities); and the other one who had excellent financial connections. Both have now been seated on the board.

Often the founder of a growing company will come to a point in the development of the business where they need help—lots of it. Sometimes they turn to the banker, the accountant or the lawyer. Each professional comes with invaluable expertise—and most times the company is paying for it. To confuse their consulting role with the governance role can lead to problems, and any CEO who offers both a board seat and a consulting contract to the same individual should be aware that this may not be the best value, but, it is one way to start. A wiser use of these professional relationships is to use them as a source of referrals for new, independent members of your board.

Another small technology company we interviewed said they used a formal process to analyze the strengths and weaknesses of the current board members. Although they had no standing committee, as a group they created the classic grid of what they had and what they were looking for. At a full board meeting, in open session, the members tossed out names of people they knew or had heard about. That process yielded about fifty names, which were narrowed down to ten by the chairman and a senior director. They then made personal contact with each of them, and narrowed it down to the final candidates. Here, this small board did all of the work together, from the grid to the sourcing of the names, making initial contacts, and conducting personal interviews. It is the same process as is used in the big leagues, just less formal, more hands-on and without the assistance (or cost) of a national search firm.

WHY DIDN'T THEY CHOOSE ME?

Interviewing for a board seat is not as random as interviewing for a job. By the time your name has surfaced on an internally developed short list, or has been presented as part of a retained search, you are in some pretty sharp company. Candidates who might be turned down because of a glaring gap in their resume, a negative reference by a former employer or a social gaffe of significant proportions, simply don't make it into the interview pool. So, rest assured, if you have been contacted about your interest in a seat, or have actually been interviewed for one, you have received a professional compliment.

However, you are not the only person being interviewed. Understand that you are one of three or four other outstanding candidates. If it doesn't work out, you've still made an important, personal contact and enjoyed a thought-provoking meal with a bright CEO. No harm done.

If a search firm presented you, then take the opportunity to inquire of them why you were not selected this time, and to reaffirm your interest in future opportunities. In the case of the CEO who interviewed candidates for his pharmaceutical company, we asked him about the individuals he did not select. He said that the two who were not chosen also interviewed very well—and could have been good additions except for the competition, and for their apparent lack of P&L or CEO type experience. (Note, however, that the academic selected also had no P&L experience.)

The key point is that not being selected is often not personal—and certainly not a negative reflection on the candidate. Much of this is being in the right place at the right time—with the right credentials—and the right personal fit.

THERE IS, HOWEVER, ONE WAY TO FAIL THE INTERVIEW PROCESS

You are being interviewed because you have already demonstrated your professional skills, expertise, and social adeptness. However, you only know what you know. By definition, you have not yet served on a corporate board, so that is the one area where you could still put your foot in it, as they say.

A CEO shared this unfortunate example with us. A mid-cap company was interviewing candidates for an open director seat. They had identified a gentleman with prior experience running the subsidiary of a large-cap company in a related industry. He knew the retail business and had demonstrated profit and loss experience. All the signs were there for a good interview.

However, his own remarks soon made it clear that he had absolutely no knowledge of corporate governance or what the responsibilities of the board might be, as opposed to those of management. When asked for his ideas on the composition of a perfect board, he replied that it should include three or four of the company's top senior managers, their lawyer, their banker, plus two or three independent directors. Grade: F.

A savvy candidate for any board of directors should, at a minimum, be visiting the National Association for Corporate Directors (NACD) and accessing their resources on director duties and professionalism before attending the interview.

NATIONAL SEARCH FIRMS SEEKING TO PLACE A NEW GENERATION OF CORPORATE DIRECTORS

Our research included discussions with several partners actively involved in building the board search practices within their national firms. They have a unique perspective on the process. It is hard to discover what percentage of all the directors seated in any given year are seated through an executive search firm. Estimates ranged from fifteen to twenty-five percent. However, we do know that the major search firms often are involved in placing the candidates that have star power and they frequently conduct searches on behalf of Fortune 1000 boards. They also are privileged to have access to thousands of resumes on potential candidates because of the databases maintained by their executive recruiting counterparts. They have a good handle on what the inventory of potential candidates looks like and how you might stack up.

> Tectonic changes have occurred in the boardrooms, and they affect profoundly how Board members are now recruited.
>
> Charles King, Partner, Korn/Ferry

We asked about the broad trends or changes they see taking place in the boardroom and how that might affect candidates being placed in the next few years:

- **Less emphasis on CEOs** There are fewer seats held by CEOs. Some claim that the availability of CEOs, in the director candidate pool, has dropped perhaps by fifty percent because CEOs are beginning to recognize their own limitations. And because their boards of directors are limiting the number of outside boards their CEOs can serve on. Years ago—and, unfortunately, still in some circles—a CEO would serve on five or six outside boards and still try to run their own company. Today, the operating principles of many companies limit their CEOs to no more than two outside boards.

- **Prior board experience** While not always a must-have, most boards are still looking for someone who has had some prior experience. We all have to start somewhere, but you can better your chances by getting valuable board experience on a first class non-profit board—preferably where you will meet CEOs from target companies.

- **Diversity** This remains an issue for many companies. According to the Gender Diversity Index (for more information visit their site at 2020WOB.com) in 2014 only 18% of seats in the Fortune 1000 boardrooms were occupied by women. Each of these companies had an average of 1.8 women on the board, meaning a significant portion still had just one. Other studies indicate that as the size of the corporation decreases, the likelihood that no woman or minority will be serving on the board increases. Many directors noted that diversity has become a business imperative and any nominating committee or CEO who has not aggressively sought diversity— not just in gender or race, but also in experiences, education, age, and perspective— is not serving their company well.

The hard part may not be in finding diverse talent...

One of the biggest challenges for the board is not in the recruiting process, but in what happens after that individual has been seated at the table. To be effective, diversity must be assimilated into the fabric of the board, including its activities and culture. Jay Cowles suggests that such a process requires strong leadership from the CEO—and greater involvement by the nominating committee members in making absolutely certain that the new board member is welcomed warmly, encouraged repeatedly, and coached to become an effective member. Too often the token woman, or minority, can be seen standing by the coffee station alone or left to take the last seat at the luncheon table. That isolation begins to wear on the new director and causes withdrawal and reluctance to participate in social events and in the critical boardroom discussions. Every effort has to be made to welcome questions, and encourage participation from new directors. If there appears to be an area where the director doesn't understand a particular business issue or topic, then it is up to the CEO who must arrange for individual tutorials—on a quiet, private basis, with the same discretion and courtesy as would be granted any other member of the board. To extend the offer for a director to join—and then not to become effective—is a failing not only of the CEO, but of every board member in the room.

For a cautionary tale, read the article that appeared in Fortune, June 15, 2015, detailing the woes at Quicksilver. Board member Elizabeth Dolan, former CMO of Nike, resigned from the board accusing the other directors (all of whom were men) or "excluding me from crucial board discussions and votes" effectively preventing her from fulfilling her role.

- **Celebrity status** Many boards want a marquee player, a name that is instantly recognizable within their industry or among the retail public that buys their products. Even athletic heroes are getting into the boardroom because their names and their achievements are attractive to customers. So, if you have out of the ordinary, exceptional public successes that may be just your ticket. Several directors and CEOs suggested that board members and employees love the idea of having a celebrity on their board. It can bring excitement to the board table, visibility to the company, and prestige to the listing of directors on the inside back cover of the annual report. It is helpful when the individual celebrity also brings substance, experience, and some business knowledge to the company, but that hasn't always been the case.

- **Financiers** Although the gold rush brought on by the Internet bubble has long passed, companies continue to look for individuals who have established connections with premier venture capital funds and significant individual or institutional investors.

- **Functional specialists** As business becomes more complex, it becomes even more important to have certain directors aboard with a deeper, narrow area of expertise to complement the broader perspectives on the board—e.g., technology, finance, marketing or consumer products. Candidates who have distinguished themselves in their specialty, if not their industry, still have a chance at positioning themselves for service as a director.

- **Periodic review of board member performance** Just as the selection process is critical to an effective board, a periodic review of the performance of existing board members is also necessary. These are becoming more commonplace. There are numerous cases where ineffective board members have hung on for too long—they were in failing health, out of touch with the marketplace, obsessive over their pet project or the way things were, or they had become disruptive to an effective governance process in the board room. Their continued presence creates a powerful argument for the need for a new generation of directors. The use of a periodic evaluation tool provides the board with an opportunity to confront these issues directly.

SUMMARY

Most corporations use a variation of the grid process to determine what they are looking for in their next member of the board. Every year, at least eight to ten thousand vacancies will occur as current directors resign or retire or new seats are added to meet the challenges of a growing organization. CEOs will work from a short list of qualified candidates, interviewing only a select few. Will your name make it onto that short list?

8

GETTING YOUR NAME ON THE SHORT LIST

> The whole process of getting on a board is like a delicate dance. The timing, the tempo, and even the rhythms of the company and the candidate have to be in sync to make it work.
>
> Joe Foster, Founder & retired CEO, Newfield Explorations, who has served on the boards of seven publicly traded companies

When a board is actively looking to add a new member or re-place one who is retiring, it never looks at all the qualified candidates. Never. Why not? Because it doesn't know who they are. Boards only choose from the candidates that they are aware of, the ones who have made it onto their short list. There are only three ways to get on that list: a personal referral, a professional referral, or through individual visibility. In each of these three instances, an intermediary is involved. Someone who knows you. Someone who acts, in a manner of speaking, as your broker.

In this pivotal chapter we will evaluate your current short list quotient, provide concrete suggestions for improving it, and intro-duce you to four brokers who made the connection to a corporate board for their talented friend or colleague. We'll also discuss a common approach that *does not work*—and the results may sur-prise you.

YOUR INDIVIDUAL SHORT LIST QUOTIENT

The goal of this self-assessment is to evaluate how likely you are to be asked to join a corporate board *today*. Understanding the process from the perspective of the board, as discussed in Chapter Seven, revealed that a short list of three to five candidates is derived from a larger list of ten or more possibilities. Therefore, to achieve your goal of service on a corporate board, you must first become a name on a list of many possible candidates; then you must make the cut to be one of the top three they are considering; and, finally, after a process of interviewing, personal references and research, you must be the one selected to become a director.

The following exercise is designed to reveal your chances at making it onto that first list of possible candidates to be approached about their interest in serving on the board. Answer each question quickly, and jot down the first few names that come to mind:

I. INDIVIDUAL VISIBILITY: HOW DO OTHERS BECOME AWARE OF YOU?

1. List the professional organizations of which you are currently an active member:

2. Name the professional conferences or industry events that you attended in the last 12-18 months:

3. Name the events at which you have spoken or participated as a panelist or industry expert in the last 12-18 months:

4. Name the professional, industry or trade publications (blogs, twitter feeds, e-magazines, online newsletters, magazines, newspapers, trade rags, etc.) in which you have been quoted, or your name or picture has appeared, or in which you have authored an article, in the last 12-18 months:

5. Summarize your online and social media presence. In what online communities are you an active contributor? What does your LinkedIn profile say about you as a potential board member?

6. List the community organizations in which you are an active participant:

7. For those community organizations listed above, briefly describe or list the events, meetings, etc. during the last 12-18 months in which you have had a leadership role:

II. PROFESSIONAL REFERRALS: WHO KNOWS YOU?

8. List the three most talented attorneys you know:

9. List the three most talented accounting professionals you know:

10. List your personal banker and your three favorite commercial bankers:

11. List three investment bankers you would call if you needed to buy or sell a company:

12. List three members of the venture capital community you could call if you wanted to secure first or second round financing for a company:

13. List the last three executive recruiters that contacted you about an opportunity:

14. List the three executive recruiters that you would call if you needed to hire an executive for your company:

15. List the three (or fewer) non-profit/charitable organizations to which you made a personal contribution last year; the amount; and the name of one or more of their board members:

16. Name the congressman that represents your district; the two senators from your state; your governor; and at least one other elected state official. Now, which of these officials have you met personally?

III. PERSONAL REFERRALS: WHO RECOMMENDS YOU?

17. List three to five individuals who have used you as a professional reference in the last 12-18 months:

18. List three to five individuals that you have referred to executive recruiters in the last 12-18 months:

19. Describe the last two or three referrals you have made that have resulted in new business for another company or professional? (E.g. referrals of tax or audit work, commercial loans, litigation, consulting projects, etc.)

20. Name three to five individuals you know (personally) that currently serve on a corporate board. List the boards they serve on:

21. List three to five companies on whose board you would like to be a director. Name the chairman and two or three other directors on each of those boards:

22. For the companies and directors named in (question 21 above), name someone you know that is an employee, acquaintance or colleague of that individual or business:

RESULTS: ASSESSING YOUR INDIVIDUAL SHORT LIST QUOTIENT

First, don't panic. There is no such thing as a perfect score or a right answer on this test—just a revealing and highly personal look at the results of the time you have invested in creating and maintaining your professional network.

The purpose of the exercise is not to have the most impressive list of names, or even a single name, under every question. In fact, most people don't. Depending on how new you are to your career, how active, or how senior, will determine how many questions you may have left blank. It is interesting to note, however, that *current directors* we have asked to complete this test could answer almost every question. These are people who know how to network!

Manley started his started his career as the executive director of a non-profit organization struggling to make ends meet in an urban setting. Most companies and civic leaders had written the organization off as a non-player. But Manley knew there was a huge role for his organization to play in getting job-training programs up and running for companies desperate for entry-level workers. Through hard work, constant leveraging of private and government funds, and sheer determination, he got the program going and it became a success. But it was not the success of the program as much as it was the way he handled himself in the innumerable meetings he held with civic leaders, state and local government officials and school administrators. His determination, his candor, his unbelievable commitment to the highest standards of training, and his passion for helping kids and corporate America at the same time, brought him to attention of the powerful people in the state. He was soon appointed to a major state office, and then joined a prestigious financial institution, keeping his commitment to non-profit efforts by being a very visible presence at fundraisers. As soon as he was settled into the financial services company, several of the executives who had worked with him at both the non-profit and government called. He got his first invitation to join a corporate board. Now he sits on seven boards, and turns down invitations by other CEOs frequently.

It may help to think of these three areas as concentric circles. The outermost circle is **Individual Visibility.** This is where, from a distance, others can observe your actions and results without knowing you personally. The next circle is that of **Professional Referrals.** Here, different professionals that you have interacted with during your career have had a chance to watch you in action, forming an opinion of your abilities as an executive or a member of the community. Finally, the smallest circle is that of **Personal Referrals.** These are individuals that have known you long enough, and well enough, to vouch personally for your character and ability. It certainly could include some of the people for whom you have worked, and some of the people who have worked for you. By definition, this inner circle is just a handful of folks, but, as we will see, their personal referral counts for a lot in the boardroom.

We'll go back over each of these three areas with you now, explain their significance, and help you assess where you can quickly generate results with some focused effort.

INDIVIDUAL VISIBILITY

Katherine was the president of a subsidiary for a large public company in the Southeast. She understood the role of the trade press and made an effort to return their calls promptly, helping them to meet deadlines, and taking care to provide factual information they could use. Often, she spoke on background or took the time to listen to their ideas and help them validate a story or point them in a better direction.

Over time, this investment paid off and Katherine became a frequent panelist at industry conferences organized by various publishers. She was also willing to speak at events with suppliers or customers and do the rubber-chicken circuit. She won several awards and, after almost ten years in the industry, was one of the names people knew.

After participating as a panelist for a financial analyst conference, she was approached by a member of the audience. He had recently taken on a senior role for a company that was not a direct competitor of her current employer, but shared many of the same suppliers and industry challenges. They were in the midst of some management changes, including a search for two new members of the board. He wanted to open a discussion with her about the company and explore her possible interest in serving on the board.

The candidate had never met the CEO, chairman, or any member of the board. However, they were aware of her credentials and position because of her visibility as an individual with an established profile at industry events.

An influential member of their senior team acted as the broker, making the initial approach, educating her on the company, and sounding out her level of interest. His recommendation initiated the delicate dance that led to her first seat on a corporate board.

Do you have the visibility within your industry so that this could happen to you? Well, how did you score on Section I: Individual Visibility? Questions 1-7 are designed to evaluate your personal visibility in your chosen industry or community.

Questions 1-4 address your activity level in professional organizations. These may be industry wide organizations such as the Information Technology Action Alliance (ITAA), or the Association of Fine Furniture Manufacturers; or they may be based on a skill set such as the Arizona State Society of Certified Professional Accountants (ASCPA) or the American Bar Association. You may be involved in specific task forces or committees to set standards or advocate for legislation affecting your industry or trade group or you could commit the time to serve as an officer of the organization.

As you review your responses against the goal of corporate board service, what is important is not the number of organizations, but the quality and visibility of your participation. Clearly, you must first do a superior job at whatever task you have taken on. However, if you are going to do the work, it may as well be in a role that gets noticed. Yes, this is Networking 101, but the lessons are worth repeating:

- Select no more than one professional organization and one community organization in which you are willing to be an active, exceptionally committed and productive member. This usually requires a three-year commitment, personal time and money, so be strategic in your selection.

- The organization you select should be populated with individuals that you admire and would like to emulate. In this case, they should be directors or CEOs of corporations.

- Take on something meaningful and execute it successfully. Head the conference. Raise the money. Open the new headquarters. Hire the next Executive Director. Whatever high visibility task you take on, do it well.

- Meet people. Sit with someone new at each meeting. Send thank-you notes, articles, refer some business. Introduce a friend or executive they've wanted to meet. Be the contact you are hoping to make. Your turn will come. First, you give. Then, you get.

- Cultivate the press. Be the spokesperson for the group, emcee the event, and introduce the guest speaker. Raise your profile. And, while you are at it, do some good. Pull your weight.

- If all this sounds exhausting, take another look at your answer to question 7. Don't volunteer for things you hate. Turn one of your passions into the vehicle that raises your profile. The press is always looking for execs that also climb mountains, save whales or turn empty lots into Little League ballparks. Spend your time on what you care about.

My advice? Get on the local business community dinner circuit. Read the business journal, follow the news. Put on that name badge and network. I can't recommend you if I have never met you.

Gary Liebl, founding president, Orange County
Chapter of the National Association of Corporate Directors

PROFESSIONAL REFERRALS

As an executive, you are interfacing with different professional colleagues and associates every day. You may not have given much thought to the impression you are creating, but they have. Over the course of your career, you have left an indelible image upon the employees, bosses, suppliers, and customers of every transaction you have been a party to. Questions 8-16 are designed to make this process visible to you and cause you to consider those professionals that may be in a position to recommend you to the CEO or Chairman of your first corporate board.

You may have left many of these questions blank. You may have not had an opportunity to interface with some of these individuals, but these are the professionals that populate the world of the CEO or director. That is why it is important for you to get to know them, and for them to have a favorable impression of you and your work product. When a board search is initiated, the directors don't ask their barber or their personal trainer for ideas. They mention it to their investment banker, their outside counsel, a fellow director, or the partner on their audit or consulting engagement. That's who they know. So, that's who you need to know.

Cole accepted his first seat on a corporate board four years ago. He was in his mid-forties and on the verge of being bored for the first time in his life. Earlier that year he had sold his company to one of the leading manufacturers in his space. It had been an incredible ten years and he had loved every difficult minute of it. Starting the company from scratch, designing the initial product offering, competing with the established players, now and then scoring a big win. But the industry was consolidating and he had sold out when the time was right.

The transaction process had been intense and deliberate. He had hired a really bright M&A team and they all put the hours in to get the best deal done. His outside counsel had been by his side throughout the entire process, and they all enjoyed a big bash in Vegas with their spouses after the deal closed.

Several months later, Cole got a call from the lead attorney. As it turned out, he was now working on the initial public offering of a company in Arizona and they were looking to put together a board. The CEO had turned to him for suggestions, asking "Who is the brightest guy you have represented in the last year?"

The board needed industry background and hands-on experience in managing the challenges of an aggressive young company in a wide-open market. His attorney thought Cole fit the bill. He cautioned that this role was going to take a lot of time and energy. The company was in a high growth mode, would soon be public, and had a management team that was pretty green.

Cole had never really considered serving as a director, but because of his relationship with the attorney, agreed to meet for steaks and sound it out. Thirty days later, the delicate dance was completed and Cole became a director. Ninety days later, the company went public.

Can a story like Cole's happen to you? It can if you make an on-purpose effort, over time, to acknowledge the importance of these professionals and their sphere of influence. Review your answers to questions 8-14 and see where you need to fill in the gaps in your network. Make it a point to use one lunch a month to maintain your professional circle of associates who are not employed by your company.

What about questions 15 and 16? Charities? Politics? You'd be surprised. First, no one has to spend more time networking than development directors and politicians. They keep great records of everyone who has ever contributed a nickel, and they remember those who wrote a generous check or stepped up to help in a pinch. If you are going to make a donation to a cause that is meaningful to you, make it count. Don't give $100 to ten environmental groups, choose one that you feel passionate about and write a thousand dollar check. Ask for a lunch with the executive director of the group and a prominent member on their board. Present the donation in person. Tell them how much you admire their work. They'll remember you.

Does your industry or trade association lobby for legislation that could improve your business? Get on the committee and make a difference. Go to Washington and make the case to your senator. Lead your group's delegation to the state house and meet with the governor and key aides. Know the people who make things happen in the political structure of your community. Return their phone calls when they call about a political appointment or want to run something by you. Let them owe you one. Then, when you need an introduction to the CEO of a major corporation in their district they'll make it happen. (A word to the wise: most savvy corporate citizens have friends on both sides of the aisle. No need to put all your eggs in one basket.)

Attorneys, bankers, consultants, legislators, accountants, recruiters—these may be tangential players to your core business. They can also be primary brokers in the subtle system of referrals that gets your name onto a short list of candidates for an open board seat.

PERSONAL REFERRALS

This is where the heavy lifting gets done. One director we interviewed described the difference between a professional referral and a personal one. The professional referral is similar to a mentor referral—I know this guy, I've told him what to do, and you might be interested in looking at him. The personal referral is similar to a broker approach—I know this woman, she is brilliant, skilled, a great team player and she could make incredible contributions to your board. It is the willingness of your broker to not only vouch for you with his personal recommendation, but his commitment to see that you have an opportunity to put your credentials to work serving a company that needs you. It is a sales job, as opposed to a simple referral.

If an attorney or consultant happens to mention your name as one of three ideas she has for board candidates, there is little personal risk involved. If the CEO asks her, "Hey, do you know this guy? I'd like a chance to meet him." There is not much downside to making the introduction and letting them take it from there. If it works out, she has a chit on her side of the ledger—a simple referral.

However, if a director or colleague of the chairman says, "I know who would be perfect for the board. Let's talk to Charles Smith." Now he or she is at risk. Charles had better turn out to be a) qualified, b) interested, and c) socially reliable. This has been a sale, and it has put the broker in the middle, responsible for the success of bringing the company and the candidate together.

This is a key point, as the door will swing both ways over time. You must be thoughtful and careful about whom you merely refer as opposed to whom you broker; and you must be careful about how you respond when you have been referred or when you are being brokered.

You can be certain that your phone does not ring at random. Someone, somewhere, has put himself or herself on the line to introduce you to this opportunity. Handle with care. Some obvious, but important, things to remember:

- Respond promptly to text messages, voice mails and e-mails. Don't let correspondence languish unanswered for days. You appear out of control and disinterested and your broker appears ineffective if they cannot even get a return phone call.

- Carefully consider each opportunity presented. If you have done your homework ahead of time, strategically managing your journey into the boardroom up to this point, then chances are that the seat is worth serious consideration.

- Agree to an initial meeting or phone call. Be prepared. (The interview and offer process will be covered in detail in Chapter Nine).

- If you decline, do so graciously and within a day or two of the initial meeting. Offer to refer them to another candidate. They may already have ten others on a list and not need your help, but you never know.

- Be certain to follow up with the person who referred or is brokering you, through a phone call or note (and, no, these haven't gone out of style) to express your appreciation. Keep them informed of how the opportunity is progressing or if you have taken yourself out of the process. Let them know that you are interested in future openings that come their way, and clarify why this opportunity was—or wasn't—the best match for you.

- If you are interested, but the company declines to continue the process, be gracious. If they are speaking with ten possibilities, only one will get the nod and the other nine of you will get a no. Keep in touch with the CEO or chairman contact you have just made. There will always be another board.

- Be certain that, no matter what the outcome, you have cast a positive reflection back on the individual that recommended you. In this delicate dance, whether you lead or follow, don't step on any toes.

With that in mind, take a look at your answers to questions 17-19. These should remind you of who currently thinks of you as a source of referrals for their business, professional contacts or employment references. This is a great place to start. If you have established yourself as something of a rainmaker, helping others to find an entrée into an important account or expand their circle of recruits for their search business, they will remember you and be happy to return the favor.

Finally, questions 20-22 assess the level of your contacts and if you have thought strategically about companies that are likely to seat you at the table in their boardroom. If you do not personally know of anyone who is a board member, then you are early in your process or you need to focus significant effort on expanding your network. If you cannot think of several specific companies where you would like to serve, it's time to start doing a little research. Once they have been identified, you can fill in the blanks on question 22, and your preparation can begin to meet opportunity.

To better understand who does this referral business, let's take a quick look at just four of the many we met during our research. These are the kinds of folks you need to know:

> **Jack T.** Jack began as a securities and commercial law specialist for a large firm in Dallas. His first board seat was as a favor for a key client of the firm. The business was in bankruptcy and needed guidance. He did a good

job and soon developed a taste for the role of a director. Over the last two decades, he has served on seven public boards. Almost all of them have been in a crisis of some sort when Jack got the call. He has developed something of a local reputation as the 'go-to guy' when things are really in a mess. He relishes this role of boardroom catalyst, but it doesn't leave much time for additional assignments. Jack maintains a private list of solid executives that he has seen in action. They may not be aware of it, but they have impressed Jack with their performance and business instincts. Now he uses that list to fill the seats that he no longer has time for. Jack stated that he gets at least two calls a month.

Gerry B. Gerry is the consummate director. After a solid career as the CEO of several public companies, he went into an active retirement as a consultant and director. Over the past twenty years, he has served on more than fifteen public and private boards, in addition to numerous charitable and educational institutions. In his own words, "The very best people are asked to serve more often than they have time for." Gerry keeps an active file of individuals he has met over the years that he can refer to the many companies that inquire after his services. Gerry says that he gets several calls a week. He enjoys being able to make these connections for other people, and the stature and recognition as a power broker this brings.

Jeff B. Jeff is in his late fifties. He was the managing partner of a public accounting firm in the Northeast for twenty years. That gave him a broad exposure to client companies across a spectrum of industries and geographies. During his tenure, the rules of his profession regarding independence did not allow him to accept any of the board seats offered him over the years. Recently, he left the firm to work as a senior financial executive for a large Korean company. He sits on three public boards, and cannot accept another seat due to time constraints. However, he receives two or three inquiries a month. He enjoys responding to these calls, understanding the needs involved, and giving them a name or two.

Jane H. Jane began her career in academics, but her love of politics soon attracted her to several major federal agencies where she played key roles. In each assignment she excelled, and her outgoing nature, her ability to engage in collegiality with men and women at all levels of government and business, her work ethic and her capacity to exercise discretion eventually led to her most sensitive position as a close advisor to the President of the United States. Along the way she made excellent connections. As a faculty member and a scholar, she has a wide network of relationships and she has been an excellent mentor to many, helping them position themselves to get top appointments in government and seats in corporate boardrooms. When deciding whether to mentor someone, she weighs the investment of her time against the possible outcome. Can this individual perform in the boardroom? Is the individual close enough to the top of their organization? Does the individual have extraordinary abilities? Has the person made major presentations or written significant articles? Does the person have a sense of humor and balanced perspective? If any of these attributes are missing, that's one less person on her list.

George P. George founded a venture capital firm twenty years ago and has been a prominent funder in a major Midwest city, working with most of the emerging companies in the multi-state region. He has watched executives develop their styles, create visions, hone their skills and earn the respect of their peers. With every company he has worked, he has collected a list of the talented executives and professional support staff and put the list into his database. Today he has over 18,000 names and copious notes about individuals who could be excellent candidates for a management position or a board seat. By watching people work, share information, and participate in creating a company, he has a sixth sense for picking people for the right position. George is active in community organizations; he supports groups of entrepreneurs, and watches the political landscape carefully, going into action whenever legislation affecting his business is needed. His knowledge of the business community and his network of executives is dominant and he is the type of person you need to know—either through your company visibility or by working on community projects and activities with which he is associated.

WHAT DOES NOT WORK?

Sometimes a scientist learns the most from the experiments that fail. Let us tell you the one approach that individuals and organizations have used time and time again that ought to work, but it doesn't. We recommend that you do not attempt it. It could be called the direct approach or the frontal assault.

> No one gets on a board by saying they want to get on a board.
>
> William H. Gray, III, President of United Negro College Fund and board member of eight publicly traded companies

To many of you, this will appear counter-intuitive. In business, we are used to being rewarded for our aggressiveness, our determination, our persistence, and our ability to define the target and go out and get it. Even in the most avant-garde corporations we visited, access to the boardroom was still on an invitation-only basis. The atmosphere, while congenial, still maintained a bit of formality. And these were the technology companies in the West. You can be assured that the financial institutions and utility companies we interviewed on the East Coast or the manufacturing concerns of the Midwest were all quite formal and stubbornly resistant to any effort to thrust a candidate upon them. It simply does not work that way.

We did not encounter one instance where a director obtained their seat on the board by pursuing it directly. No one that we know got into the boardroom by calling or contacting the CEO directly to ask for a seat, by sending e-mails to other directors, by contacting the human resource department, or by registering with an placement organization that was supposed to get them on board. Nope. Not even one.

(An exception to this finding would be instances where shareholders used their proxy access to nominate their own slate of directors for the board. This used to be unheard of, but is now becoming more common in companies that are in severe distress or in serious conflict with a major shareholder or interest group. We did not encounter this situation during our research.)

If you are used to making things happen your way, on your timetable, and you find this obscure, indirect, subtle approach frustrating, then you probably won't enjoy the role of director. Take this to be an important personal clue about yourself. Spend your time and energy doing something more direct. You'll make a great VP of Sales. But take it from us: the path to the boardroom is unmarked and silent. Someone else has to open the door and ask you in.

SUMMARY

By now it is clear that you need more than just financial acumen and a successful track record in business to be on the short list for the next board seat. You need to be known: known by your visibility as an individual in your industry or community; known by professionals who will mention you as a possible candidate; or known by someone with the influence to personally refer you to the chairman, CEO or a director on the board. This means you need a broker, a mentor, a trusted friend or advisor in a position of influence who can act as an intermediary, making the necessary introductions, referrals or recommendations. In this delicate dance onto the short list, you need a partner. So, who do you know?

9

THE OFFER: MAKING A MATCH THAT'S RIGHT FOR YOU

Now we're down to the home stretch. After your name gets on that short list, the next step is the critical call. It can range from a simple phone message, left by a CEO asking you to breakfast to talk about her company, to a facilitation meeting by your broker and the CEO, to a call from the director who serves as chair of a governance committee. Next is the interview, then the offer, and finally you have to make a decision. Will this be your first seat on a corporate board? We'll tell you what to expect from each step on the dance floor, and then leave you with a checklist for performing that all-important gut-check before you pick up the phone to accept your new role.

THE INTERVIEW

The interview will be much less focused than a traditional job interview, more congenial, and more sophisticated. This is the point at which the CEO and other directors present will be trying to validate your skills, achievements, and bullet points in your resume. But, more importantly, they also will be trying to determine the fit between you, the CEO, the corporation's culture, and the other members of the board. How will you contribute in the boardroom? How resourceful, supportive and helpful will you be outside the boardroom? How will you relate to the other directors? How will they relate to you? What will the financial analysts think when they learn you are the newest member of the board?

As with any interview, you must be completely prepared to meet with the CEO, having done your comprehensive research on the company by reading the annual reports, visiting the website, accessing the five most recent SEC filings, filtering through the investment information published by any firm that covers the stock, and gathering any informal information you can from your networks about the company, the executives, and the other directors.

At the interview you should be well dressed, but not overly dressed, relaxed, confident, respectful, energetic, and eager to learn about their expectations for new directors. Every answer you give should be focused as to how your expertise could be an opportunity for their company. For example: how your experiences translate into getting a better handle on the supply chain; how your ideas for identifying new markets might help the company grow; what experiences you've had in exploring new technologies; what contacts you have that might assist the company in seeking new alliances or whatever other challenges may appear.

A few words of common sense: don't be pompous, preachy, or eager to tell them how much you know about absolutely everything. Rather, position your energy and ideas as additional resources for the company. Remember, this is not a job interview. You are not going to work at the company. Reveal, by the nature of your discussion, that you are aware of this important distinction between the role of management and the role of the board. Directors do not run companies, they represent the stakeholders of the organization they serve, and they guide senior management. (Head back to Chapters One and Two if this is still fuzzy in your mind.)

THE OFFER

Let's assume you have aced the initial interviews, gone on to meet most of the directors on the board. Now the chairman says he would like to extend an invitation to sit on the board. This declaration may come as part of the closing remarks during your last interview or it may come from the corporate secretary or general counsel in a follow-up conversation covering the details.

In many of the larger public corporations, you won't get a letter confirming the offer, a non-compete agreement or any of the other formal documents you've come to expect as part of the job interview process. The feeling is often more one of a "gentlemen's agreement". However, it is perfectly acceptable to ask for a written summary of the details you have discussed along with a confirmation of the D&O liability coverage that will be extended to you upon acceptance. On or around your first board meeting, you will receive a few forms to complete, primarily regarding director payments (they'll need your social security number), and the designation of beneficiary for any insurance policies, deferred compensation plans or other benefits.

Thorough package, in writing, offered some directors

Another seasoned CEO, at a smaller company, says he makes the offer by inviting the candidate back for another meeting and then providing them with a letter detailing the expectations of the board, the expectations a new director should reasonably have, the compensation arrangements, and information about any other company benefits.

In the smaller companies (and even in some of the mid-cap companies we spoke with), it is likely that the CEO will personally make the offer to you to join the board. Occasionally, that happens at the end of your first and only interview. Certainly you will express gratitude and appreciation at being asked to join such a distinguished group of individuals, and such an outstanding organization. Then you should take a deep breath and tell the CEO that you will get back to her in a few days after you have had time to reflect on the opportunity and balance it against your present commitments.

Always give yourself a little extra time, and the possibility of a gracious withdrawal from the process, if necessary. If nothing else, the extra time will give you a chance to get the necessary approvals from your company, your boss or your attorney and to privately celebrate by calling your spouse, your mother or your mother-in-law to tell them what a success you're about to be. Or, more likely, take time to regroup and deal with any last minute questions and concerns that have surfaced.

HOW MUCH?

> The invitation is mainly flattery...and, at least with the smaller companies, there won't be a hell of a lot of money.
>
> A director of several companies and mutual funds

At a minimum, your compensation as a director should include an annual retainer, in cash or in stock grants, or a combination of both. A pleasant addition to most packages is a "signing bonus", an initial grant of company stock. This is usually equal to the amount awarded annually to all directors. In one company we spoke with it was just two hundred shares; in others it was thousands of shares.

In addition to the annual retainer, the company often pays for attendance, ranging from $250 up to $5000 per meeting. Some companies have a different pay scale for committee meetings, generally paying less for those than for meetings of the full board. Other companies have a different rate for directors who participate by telephone—typically less than the fee for in-person attendance.

Once you become a chairperson of a committee, you can expect an additional annual stipend or retainer, because you will now be working harder than the rest of the committee members. In companies with sophisticated governance practices, the committee chairs are rotated on a regular basis.

A common theory today is that directors make better decisions when their financial interests are more closely aligned with the shareholders they represent. Therefore, many board compensation packages include restricted stock units (RSUs) that vest over time, or when certain financial performance metrics have been achieved. Other directors report receiving outright stock grants, or stock options that vest over 1-4 years.

Compensation varies greatly by industry and size of the organization. Each year, several studies are published which cumulate and analyze this data for public companies. (Spencer Stuart makes this information available, as does Korn Ferry.)

WHAT YOU SEE IS WHAT YOU GET

Unlike the offers made in job interviews, this is not an opening volley across the bow, just to get things started. This is it. There is no negotiating the director compensation plan. The fees are set forth in the company's proxy statements that are filed with the SEC. While they are not set in stone, they are public information, requiring at least a company resolution, if not stockholder approval, in order to change the director compensation plan. So what is offered is what you are going to get.

All for one and one for all

One executive we interviewed agreed that there could be no dickering with the offer. However, his was a story with a slightly different ending.

When offered a seat on the board of a relatively new company, he realized that the current director compensation plan was unacceptable. However, he was intrigued by the opportunity, had been personally recommended by another board member for whom he had great respect, and was genuinely interested in helping the company, even though he would not do it at the compensation currently offered. He decided to let the company know, graciously, that the offer was out of line, clearly under the market. The executive politely offered a copy of his own company's director compensation package and suggested they might want to match that.

The company issuing the invitation did review the package, revised their compensation plan for all directors, had the revisions approved, and then raised their fees. Our executive joined the board and was an instant hero, among the other directors, who now received the benefit of an improved compensation package that more closely matched the market.

The financial details of your offer should be the same as that extended for all directors. It's the authors' belief that even in the smallest companies, independent directors should be on a level playing field. However, we did learn of at least one circumstance where a director received a larger annual retainer simply because he demanded it, and the rest of the board thought his contributions to be significant enough to justify paying one person more than the others for the same work. The rationale was that this unique director brought so much more expertise, such better connections, and substantially more prestige to the company than the other directors. We hope that remains an isolated incident.

ANY FRIES TO GO WITH THAT COKE?

Most directors experience some benefits in addition to the cash retainer and stock. Almost all companies provide travel reimbursement for directors while on company business. Your expenses of getting to and from the board of director meeting will be reimbursed. As mentioned in Chapter Two, the amount varies dramatically, and you should have a personal conversation with the corporate secretary, general counsel, CEO or whoever is going to process your travel voucher to determine what is reimbursable and what is not.

Typically, your carfare or mileage expense to get to the airport or the meeting is reimbursable; as are your parking fees and toll fares, your airfare, meals during travel, your hotel room and reasonable meals taken during your time away from home. Normally, expenses for personal care, dry-cleaning, newspapers and shoe shines, and any liquor will not be reimbursed.

All companies should offer director/officer liability insurance. If they don't, that is a strong signal to decline the invitation or consider, very carefully, whether you want to associate with that company.

Some companies offer other limited insurance benefits to directors. For example, one company provides an insurance policy covering accidental death or dismemberment while traveling on company business. According to the recent surveys on board compensation, roughly ten percent of the large-cap companies offer life insurance where the director names the beneficiary to the policy. Another ten percent offer a life insurance policy that, upon death, will make a payment to a particular charity (originally of the director's choice, but now more likely to be at the mutual choice of the company and the director). Only four or five percent of these large public companies offer any form of health or medical insurance benefits for their directors.

Forty percent of the companies surveyed have matching gifts programs to match the directors' contributions to educational institutions or charitable organizations. These programs usually follow the pattern of the company foundation giving guidelines.

About seventeen percent of the companies offered to reimburse travel expenses for a director's spouse. Many companies hold annual retreats, strategy sessions, and visits to remote locations or other outings. While the trend is clearly away from spousal attendance, there are companies, especially in the Fortune 100, who still go to great expense to stage trips, dinners and other events that include directors, senior management, and their respective spouses.

THE GUT-CHECK

> The first board seat I took I did not do enough due diligence. A friend recruited me and I trusted his research and judgment. Big mistake.
>
> Venture capitalist and board member of several technology companies in the West

You have completed the interview process. You have received an invitation to join the board. All that remains is to pick up the phone and accept or decline. Before you touch that cell phone, stop and consider your answers to the questions on the following checklist. (...with thanks to Gary Liebl, Founding Chairman of QLogic Corporation and the Forum for Corporate Directors. He often used the following checklist to counsel potential candidates.)

BOARD OF DIRECTOR CANDIDATE CHECKLIST

1. Does the company provide director indemnification?

2. Do they have D&O insurance? Is the policy consistent with the company's size and maturity as an organization?

3. How do I relate to the CEO? My kind of person? Do we have good chemistry?

4. Do I buy in to the company's vision? Do I understand its strategic plan? Do I have any serious reservations about where they are heading?

5. Can I determine the value systems of the CEO and his or her current board members? Are they similar? Are they compatible with my own?

6. How is my chemistry with the other board members I have met? Have I had a chance to meet them all? Do their responses to similar questions reveal a deep rift or division on the board?

7. What is the financial health of the company? Does it have a reasonable success scenario on the horizon? Do I understand its current challenges and problems?

8. Does the board have an audit committee? A compensation committee? What other formal committees are currently standing?

9. What is the company's litigation record? Does it currently have any significant outstanding lawsuits pending? Do they worry me?

10. Have I reviewed the financial statements? Recent annual and quarterly reports? Proxy statement and any SEC filings?

11. Have I personally referenced the CEO and some or all of the current board?

12. Is the remuneration for service on the board acceptable to me?

13. Is the calendar for board meetings reconcilable with my current commitments, both professionally and personally?

14. Can I spend the amount of time that will be required to be a virtual 100% contributor? Without reservation?

15. Have I made the case (verbally) for joining this board to a trusted friend or mentor? How did they reaction?

16. Have I done the same with my spouse? What was his or her reaction?

17. What do I bring to this board? Do I have the experience and skill to really make a difference here?

18. What is my *real motivation* for wanting to join this board? Is it prestige, money, the opportunity to add value, to make a difference, or?

19. Am I *excited* about joining this board?

20. *What is my gut telling me to do?*

If you have taken the time to answer, for yourself, each of the questions on this checklist—then you know what to do. If, upon reflection, you realize that your heart is not into casino gambling, and the company who invited you to join its board manufactures slot machines, than this may not be the right board seat for you. Even subtler, if you realize that several of the other board members appear to be a little arrogant, condescending, or even obnoxious during the interviewing process—know that they will only become more so after you've worked with them for a few months, or years. As with marriage, what's bad at the beginning is worse at the end. If your checklist came up with too many red flags, you need to decline the invitation.

Isn't it too late to back out now?

One director suggested the entire courting process—right up to the offer—was just like dating, and after a certain progression it is impossible to just say no. You had to go ahead and get married.

We disagree. You can, and you should, say no if you have any reservations. There are many ways you can graciously decline to serve, coming down ultimately to the old stand-by of "personal reasons"—if all else fails you. It is much better to say no before you ever get into the boardroom than to go into it with reservation, with restrictions on your ability to perform, or with personal reluctance to do your very best for the company and the shareholders.

Once a public announcement has been made that you are a new board member, it becomes very difficult to get off that board until a reasonable amount of time (e.g., a year or eighteen months) have passed. An early departure looks much worse than a last minute no during the offer process.

True, saying no may surprise the CEO after a lengthy courtship, but if it is handled professionally, it can also result in preserving a valued professional contact, or even in creating a friendship. One director we interviewed did develop last minute concerns about the company and about his ability to fit in. Wisely, he withdrew his name from consideration. He then offered the names of five other individuals that he felt could do an excellent job, and who would not be subject to the same concerns that he had. The candidate who declined eventually made two new friends— the CEO and the new director who benefited from his personal referral.

On the other hand, if your checklist was flashing with green lights, if the CEO is the brightest person you've met in the last five years, if the other board members are world-class executives, and the company is poised to revolutionize the health care industry— which just happens to be your passion—go for it! Pick up the phone and give the CEO your unqualified yes.

SUMMARY

Accepting your first seat on a corporate board is a big deal. It means you've achieved a significant goal, one you may have set for yourself years ago. Now for the fun part. It's time to prove yourself again— but this time you'll be doing so in a different arena. Representing the interests of a diverse group of stakeholders, in the service of a very interesting company, you'll be learning, thinking and making decisions at a whole new level. You'll also be broadening your business horizons, enhancing your credentials, perhaps even socking away valuable stock options in your investment portfolio. If you've chosen wisely, you'll be doing all this in the company of bright folks who work together in a cordial and professional atmosphere. What more could you want?

10

NEW ON BOARD? BECOMING PART OF THE TEAM

> Being on boards...it's like the rent you pay for the space you occupy. [Once you are successful in your own company or professionally]... serving on a board can be your way of giving back to the larger business community. It can be your greatest contribution.
>
> Mark Sheffert, Chairman and CEO, Manchester Companies
> and current or former member of thirty boards of
> publicly traded and private companies

You have accepted your first seat on a corporate board. Congratulations. The process of becoming a board member has ended. The process of serving as a director has just begun.

Someone, somewhere, took a personal interest in you and vouched for your qualifications and ability. That got you onto the short list. The chairman, CEO and several other directors have met with you and given you the nod. Now it's your turn to demonstrate that they have made the right decision. Don't forget the thank-you notes.

Before we discuss what will happen at your first meeting, you need to make room for three new things on your professional calendar: Boardroom Resources, Company and Board Meeting

Preparation, and Board Communication. These are the three areas that distinguish a good board member from an empty seat.

Boardroom Resources will enable you to lay a foundation for understanding your role as a director, generally, and are external to the board you are joining. Company and Board Meeting Preparation will establish a simple, consistent method for you to stay current on issues and trends that are specifically applicable to the company on whose board you serve. Board Communication will establish and maintain productive and professional relationships among your fellow board members and the senior management of the company. The secret is to schedule a consistent, simple process of learning, preparing, and communicating during your first year or two on the board. After that, it will be second nature. For now, you need to be on purpose about setting aside a few hours a month to get up to speed in your new role.

These three steps are designed to address the common complaints we heard about bad board members, and to reinforce the behaviors described as common to good board members by the CEOs and directors we interviewed.

Boardroom Resources

You need knowledge of the basics of corporate governance and a means to stay abreast of changes. If you already have such a foundation, skip this section. However, we have found that most of our readers do not have these basics under their belt, but are just embarrassed to ask, "To whom do I owe my fiduciary duty? What are the committee responsibilities? How does the board effectively discharge their responsibilities? How much stock do I need to buy? How candid can I be in the boardroom? Should I call the CEO with my questions ahead of the meeting or just blurt them out during the meeting?"

Purchase one or two good books on corporate governance for your library, and consider joining an organization for directors or subscribing to a journal that will allow you to keep current with director-specific issues and legislation. That will get you started. Set Google alerts for the companies or industry issues you want to stay on top of. Subscribe to just 2-3 high quality online newsletters—KPMG and Deloitte both to a good job of culling through the regulatory chaff and serving up what is really meaningful. The large securities law firms and compensation consultants also have these types of updates. Spend time on a web site—reading about companies who got into trouble and analyze where the governance process failed. There are great case studies of companies who have failed.

You need to see the broader context of what you are doing so you can be aware of changes that may affect your specific role. It's like understanding how broad movements in the Dow Jones can impact the specific stocks you invest in. Far reaching changes or pronouncements by the SEC or the AICPA, for example, recently changed the structure, composition, and responsibilities of the audit committee. This affected the board of almost every publicly held corporation in America. Because of the resources you have established, you would have heard about this, and read some background before attending your next board meeting. This would allow you to participate, intelligently, in a discussion of how this change affects your current board.

Try to commit to one book, or series, such as Jossey-Bass Business and Management series or the works of Ralph D. Ward and John Carver. We'll suggest two to get you started: Boardroom Basics: A Pocket Guide for Directors by Roger H. Ford and the National Association of Corporate Directors' Report of the NACD Blue Ribbon Commission on Director Professionalism. A quick trip to Amazon.com will show you that over four hundred fifty books have been written for directors, but many of these deal with non-profit and foundation boards or with specific issues such as CEO compensation or succession. At this point, it's enough just for you to realize those reference books are out there, if required. Schedule at least two hours or pack these in your briefcase for your next airplane ride and get this foundation reading done. You'll feel better with an established context for the boardroom and a guide to refer to.

Next, use your established relationships with the search firm of your choice to receive an annual copy of their boardroom research.

This will keep you up to date on director compensation and option plans, diversity and composition of boards and committees, and gives you a reason to stay current in their database and aware of other opportunities down the road. Spencer Stuart and Heidrick & Struggles each have their own comprehensive surveys. Korn/Ferry has an annual survey, now in its 28th year, which is very well done. Call your contacts there, or check out their websites if you'd like to start a file with this year's report.

Several organizations exist to connect and support corporate directors. Look for the local chapter of the National Association of Corporate Directors. They host seminars and conferences, which may vary in quality. Some are excellent and others tend to be over-run by service providers who want to meet you in the hopes of doing business with the company you serve!

There are excellent director seminars and short courses available at various colleges and universities around the country. Some larger corporations actually fund the tuition and attendance expenses at these courses. If time permits, it may be worth your effort to attend one of the courses at Wharton, Kellogg, or the many other colleges and universities offering a two-day to week-long curriculum.

Of course, your primary source for finding what you need to stay current will be online. BoardMember magazine is now part of the NYSE Governance Services portal. You'll want to explore that as well as the NACD site with its offerings under Director Professionalism.

COMPANY AND BOARD MEETING PREPARATION

Effective preparation requires an initial investment of your time to gain an appropriate level of understanding of the company's operations, strategies, and challenges. You will also have to develop a mechanism for an ongoing process of awareness and preparation for the formal board or committee meetings.

It is assumed that you did your homework on the company before accepting a seat on the board. Therefore, you have already met many of the directors and the CEO. You already understand the basics of the business they are in and what is expected of you as a member. Now it is time to get specific.

During our research, we encountered a wide disparity in the process by which companies orient new members to the board. At one end of the spectrum, we found CEOs who gave us a quizzical look when asked to describe the orientation process for directors. They then confessed to doing nothing more than making introductions to senior management, welcoming the new director to their first meeting, and sending them a packet with the agenda in the mail!

On the other end, we spoke with many directors and CEOs who benefited from a formal orientation process that included plant tours, an overview of key business processes by the senior management team, a review of competitors, copies of key documents from the previous business cycle, etc. New directors spent over forty hours learning about the company before ever attending their first meeting.

Your experience will probably fall between these two extremes. The important thing is to be proactive. Ask for a calendar of the scheduled meetings for the coming year, and an introduction to whoever coordinates the activities of the board. In some companies this is the corporate counsel, in others the corporate secretary, in others it is the executive assistant to the Chairman or CEO. This is the individual who can make available to you past board packets, clippings or key articles, studies on competitors, reports made by industry analysts, etc. If the CEO who extended your invitation to the board does not offer, politely inquire if a site visit or plant tour or half-day orientation might be appropriate before attending your first meeting. Then, follow his lead. It goes without saying that whatever information is given to you needs to be thoroughly reviewed and carefully read. It's up to you to be prepared.

In addition you need specific information about your particular company's practices. Befriend the corporate secretary or the CEOs personal assistant as quickly as possible, and ask for a lesson on how to use the company ropes.

TRAVEL

What are the travel allowances for board members? If you can't get specifics, ask for a copy of the travel policy for the company and follow the policies set out for senior management. If senior management doesn't travel first class, you don't travel first class.

It is rare that a board member will be entertaining people on behalf of the company. But, if you find yourself getting into those circumstances, clarify the company practice *before* you make the commitment. Often, the chair of the governance or nominating committee will be meeting potential candidates for board recruitment. Expense reimbursement should be made, but there is a huge difference between dinner at Sardi's in New York City and a cup of coffee at Starbucks. Find out what the company expectations are before you pull out your credit cards.

COMPANY EVENTS

In addition to the regularly scheduled board meetings, most companies hold other events and often invite board members. As a new member, you should go. If, at the second event you are once again the only board member in attendance, conclude that the invitation was a courtesy, not a command.

At the events, your job is to learn, not lead. The CEO—or senior officer present—is in charge and you are just one more invited guest. Use the opportunity to learn more about senior management and how they relate to the other guests. Learn everything you possibly can about how the guests view the company.

If the invitation includes spouse or significant other, make an early, and relatively firm decision: either you decide this is business and you don't mix family with business, so you go alone, go early and leave early; or you may decide your style (which matches the company's style) will be to get you and your family totally involved. If in doubt, we encourage new board members to consider everything business, and unless the spouse or significant other is really going to insist on inclusion, go alone.

Just so we cover all the bases, attendance at any company event (a ballgame at Yankees Stadium, a customer event at a big conference center or a casual gathering at the local hotel bar) requires the same impeccable business etiquette as in any other business situation. If in doubt, pick up one of the great business etiquette paperbacks and do a quick read. Generally speaking, you should never use a loud voice, drink excessively, dress provocatively, make off-color remarks, or engage in braggadocio. Simply put: do nothing that would ever come back to haunt you because your mother learned of the incident as it was reported in the *Wall Street Journal*, tweeted out by a bystander, or posted on someone's Facebook.

COMPANY REQUESTS

Inevitably, as a new board member, you will receive a request for your contribution—*the raison d'etre*—why you were invited to serve on the board.

It may be a request from the chief technology officer for help looking at specific software specifications, since you know you were recruited to be the technology expert on the board.

These requests should be expected, and they should be responded to as quickly as possible. Unless you are the President of the United States (and by definition they don't serve on corporate boards— until retirement, that is), you should arrange for a response to a telephone call within twenty-four hours, either through e-mail, your assistant, or a midnight voice mail message telling the caller when you can find time to talk in detail about the request.

Board members most valuable contribution is generally information: about products and services, about strategic plans or corporate governance, about other company practices, other people and other things. Our experience is that company requests are usually the kind that can be disposed of based on your general expertise in the relevant area.

But, on occasion, the request may require you to do actual work: research an issue, make telephone calls to others, or review and examine specifications or documents. Exercise care that you are not the final reviewer or examiner, but that you are simply adding your input to the decision-making process. You cannot afford to hear in the boardroom (eighteen months later) that you, as the board member whom they relied on, told them to buy the equipment that failed or suggested the tactic that backfired before the regulatory agency.

If in doubt, before responding to a complicated request, check with the CEO and learn exactly what are the expectations for your input, how they will use it, and what other due diligence they are conducting.

If the response does require significant work on your part, consider it part of the services rendered for your board member retainer, fees or stock options. If you feel that you are being short changed because the amount of the work is significant, go back and re-read the earlier section in Chapter Two on serving as a consultant vs. a board member.

Other kinds of requests that companies often make of their board members are requests to help facilitate a meeting with a client or to recruit an executive. These are all legitimate requests—and things, hopefully, you can do quickly and efficiently for the company.

These early requests, and your responses, are the most significant in setting the tone of your relationship and role as a director outside the boardroom.

BOARD COMMUNICATION

Communication styles among boards are as unique as the CEOs that initiate them. The method is not as important as the frequency and the ease with which issues of importance to the board are made known in a timely manner. Depending on the company, this may be necessary once a quarter or even once a month. In the midst of a significant transaction or financial crisis, it could even be weekly for a short period of time.

Again, during your initial meeting or conversation with the individual responsible for board communication ask for clarity as to the preferred method. Most boards now send all their materials to an online dropbox, such as Diligent or Boardbooks. You can access, via the cloud, confidential information from past meetings and all the current minutes, etc. However, some boards still do everything in writing and send it overnight by FedEx. Others swear by weekly faxes or monthly phone conferences. Still other boards send updates by e-mail and only speak in person when attending quarterly meetings. Just be sure you are clear on what is to be expected and when. For at least the first year, do not vary from what is "regularly scheduled", if at all possible. When you have some seniority, you can request that the committee work be done via conference call or that the meetings start at 7:00 AM, instead of 8:30 so you can catch an earlier plane. But, for your first few meetings, just go along and get along. Be on time, be prepared.

Finally, into the boardroom

Your first meeting. What to expect? In many ways it is no different than the hundreds of other business meetings you have attended. It may be a little more formal, a little more stylized. In a sense, it is the "ritual" of business.

> Get yourself into the flow as quickly as possible. At the first meeting—be visible...don't sneak up the back stairs. You are there for a reason, so be proactive and ready to support the company.
>
> Larry Downes, CEO, New Jersey Resources

The parliamentary procedure, the taking of minutes, the need for motions and seconds—it can all seem a little silly and, well, strange at first, but you will get used to it.

To help you make a good start, we asked our interviewees some final questions. Here is a sampling of some of their best advice for you, the next generation of directors:

©Dave Carpenter. Used by permission.

"Your first board meeting?"

As a new director, did anything surprise you?

"Did anything surprise me? Of course! I guess I should have realized that it is similar to interviewing for a job, or even for a date. Everyone puts his or her best face forward. It had not occurred to me that the different directors I met did not get along. I had no idea that the founder of the company was going to file for divorce, and that it would precipitate a tremendous battle for control of the company, and eventually result in his resignation. Surprised? Yes, that all happened within my first few meetings. It was quite the introduction."

Former CEO and director of a
publicly held technology company

How important is preparation?

The CEO of a large public company in the Western US answered that question with this example: "After a few frustrating meetings, I finally realized [this director] looked at our board package as being just a list of what we might talk about at the meeting. He never even took the paper clip off of it until the meeting began. It made me nuts. One of the other directors finally clued him in. The package was background, it was assumed that everyone around the table had already read and understood the contents. That got the board all on the same page as management. So my advice would be, don't skimp on your preparation. Don't make everyone else go back and start at the beginning. It is embarrassing to have to direct [a new] member to the page number where the answer to his first question is typed out. Prepare!"

Thinking back to your own first experience as a director, was there anything you wish you had known ahead of time?

"Anything I wish I'd known? Well, sure. Three of us had been recruited as outside directors for a technology-based company that was pre-public. This was years ago, long before the Internet craze. The company had been in business for years, was making money, etc. Each of us had done our due diligence. After our first two meetings, we were getting ready to actually do the filing and it came to light that we would have to replace the CEO, as he had a prior felony conviction. Now, that's not one of the questions I thought to ask during my interview!"

Former chairman of public company and director

Finally, how long does it take before a new director is up to speed and contributing?

"First, take some time to understand the culture. Every board is unique. Don't bring up serious issues or challenges, for the first time ever, in front of the full board. Don't surprise, embarrass, or ambush the CEO. Use committees as a forum or outside discussions to sound an early alarm among other board members or to surface an important issue for discussion," notes John Lewis, former CEO and vice-chairman of Sun Community Bancorp. (SCBL) "When the company faces an important challenge, bring in outside information and lead a balanced discussion of the alternatives. Realize that every board has a fuzzy line between the CEO and the members he inherited, versus those he handpicked. You will need to establish your own chemistry that will allow you to be strategic, productive, and tactful—not tactical."

SUMMARY

Now, you know how to get your first seat on a corporate board.

Our intention in writing this book was to make an important capstone in your career more accessible. Together, we have established what it is that board members really do; why they do it; and the central conflict that is inherent in their role. We've given you the tools to determine if you have what it takes— the skills and the experience to contribute at the board level; and if now is the right time in your career to take on this new role. Finally, we have explained what you could do (and what someone else must do for you) to match your years of preparation with an opportunity. We discussed the board member selection process; how to get your name on the short list; what to expect in an offer; and some final advice on how to become part of the team, gracefully, when you take that first seat on a corporate board.

We hope our time together has taken the mystery out of the boardroom for you. You now understand what goes on in there, what it takes to be a good board member, and whether this is a career goal that makes sense for you. You've heard it straight from the horse's mouth—in the anecdotes, personal stories, and advice we gathered for you from the CEOs and directors of over one hundred companies in America.

Yes, the mystery is gone, but we hope the mystique remains. The allure of business in a place where the stakes are the highest, the players are the brightest, and the game is by invitation only—the allure of the boardroom. We've never tired of it. Neither will you.

SUGGESTED READING

BOOKS:

Bakewell, Thomas et al, *Claiming Your Place at the Boardroom Table; The Essential Handbook for Excellent in Governance.* 2014

Bowen, William G. *The Board Book: An Insider's Guide for Directors and Trustees,* 2012

Calderson, Nancy et al., *Women on Board: Insider Secrets to Getting on a Board and Succeeding as a Director,* 2013

Charan, Ram et al., *Boards that Lead: When to Take Charge, When to Partner, and When to Stay out of the Way.* 2013

E-NEWSLETTER:

Fleck, George, *Director Moves…Who's News in the Boardroom and C-Suite*

WEBSITES

www.boardeffect.com

www.boardmember.com

www.boardseat.com

www.broadrooms.com

www.diligent.com

www.directorsandboards.com

www.eboardmember.com

www.executiveadvisory.com

www.heidrick.com

www.kornferry.com

www.managementhelp.org

www.NACDonline.org

www.nyse.com/governance

www.C200.org

www.sec.gov—Dodd-Frank Reform and Consumer Protection Act

www.sec.gov—Sarbanes-Oxley Act

www.spencerstuart.com

www.womenintheboardroom.com

www.womenonboards.org.au

www.2020wob.com

ASSESSMENT OF PERSONAL CANDIDACY FOR BOARD SERVICE

(Answering the question, "Am I a good fit for a director's role on the board?")

SKILLS:

- Do I have specific, identifiable skills sets to bring to the table?

- Do I have a record of professional achievement?

- Can I demonstrate specific results?

- Am I "financially literate", as defined by the SEC, for Audit Committee service?

- Do I understand basic concepts of corporate governance?

TEMPERAMENT:

- Do I naturally head toward the big picture, or do I get bogged down in detail?

- Do I have patience for long-term results as opposed to this quarter's results?

- Am I a team player?

- Do I build on others' ideas, or get offended when my idea isn't adopted?

- Do I have a comfort level with the group process?

OTHER:

- Do I have an executive presence?

- Am I optimistic and upbeat?

- Do I have a known reputation for
  - Integrity?
  - Community involvement?
  - Industry leadership?

- Do I bring contacts and connections to the table?

INDIVIDUAL SHORT LIST QUOTIENT

(Answering the question, "Will my name make it onto the short list of board candidates?)

The following exercise is designed to reveal your chances at making it onto that first list of possible candidates to be approached about their interest in serving on the board. Answer each question quickly, and jot down the first few names that come to mind:

I. INDIVIDUAL VISIBILITY: HOW DO OTHERS BECOME AWARE OF YOU?

1. List the professional organizations of which you are currently an active member:

2. Name the professional conferences or industry events that you attended in the last twelve to eighteen months:

3. Name the events at which you have spoken or participated as a panelist or industry expert in the last twelve to eighteen months:

4. Name the professional, industry or trade publications (online, e-zines, newsletters, magazines, newspapers, trade rags, etc.) in which you have been quoted, or your name or picture has appeared, or in which you have authored an article, in the last twelve to eighteen months:

5. List the community organizations in which you are an active participant:

6. For those community organizations listed above, briefly describe or list the events, meetings, etc. during the last twelve to eighteen months in which you have had a leadership role:

7. Describe your three favorite non-work related activities:

II. PROFESSIONAL REFERRALS: WHO KNOWS YOU?

8. List the three most talented attorneys you know:

9. List the three most talented accounting professionals you know:

10. List your personal banker and your three favorite commercial bankers:

11. List three investment bankers you would call if you needed to buy or sell a company:

12. List three members of the venture capital community you would call if you wanted to secure first- or second-round financing for a company:

13. List the last three executive recruiters that contacted you about an opportunity:

14. List the three executive recruiters that you would call if you needed to hire an executive for your company:

15. List the three (or fewer) non-profit/charitable organizations to which you made a personal contribution last year, the amount, and the name of one or more of their board members:

16. Name the congressman that represents your district, the two senators form your state, your governor, and at least one other elected state official. Now, which of these officials have you met personally?

III. PERSONAL REFERRALS: WHO RECOMMENDS YOU?

17. List three to five individuals who have used you as a professional reference in the last twelve to eighteen months:

18. List three to five individuals that you have referred to executive recruiters in the last twelve to eighteen months:

19. Describe the last two or three referrals you have made that have resulted in new business for another company or professional (e.g. referrals of tax or audit work, commercial loans, litigation, consulting projects, etc.):

20. Name three to five individuals you know (personally) that currently serve on a corporate board. List the boards they serve on:

21. List three to five companies on whose board you would like to be a director. Name the chairman and two or three other directors on each of those boards:

22. For the companies and directors named in question 21 above, name someone you know that is an employee, acquaintance or colleague of that individual or business:

RESULTS: ASSESSING YOUR INDIVIDUAL SHORT LIST QUOTIENT

First, don't panic. There is no such thing as a perfect score or a right answer on this test—just a revealing and highly personal look at the results of the time you have invested in creating and maintaining your professional network.

The purpose of the exercise is not to have the most impressive list of names, or even a single name, under every question. In fact, most people don't. Depending on how new you are to your career, how active, or how experienced, will determine how many questions you may have left blank. It is interesting to note, however, that *current directors* we have asked to complete this test could answer almost every question. These are people who know how to network!

By reviewing your answers to each of the above sections, you can create a pretty clear picture of where your network is strong and well established and where you need to "fill in some blanks." What are you waiting for?

INDIVIDUAL ACTION PLAN

(Answering the question, "What tangible steps can I take towards my goal today?")

- Polish personal credentials and create resume reflecting senior-level skills and potential contributions to a board of directors

- Identify potential industries

- Target five companies who could be possible matches

- Research "circles of influence" at each company

- Assess ways to connect with this influential circle

- Identify CEOs and other board members who could be helpful

- Develop strategy to connect with these individuals through industry meetings, civic or charitable organizations, or informal networks

- Identify search firms who may possibly be helpful

- Create action plan and time table

CHECKLIST PRIOR TO ACCEPTING BOARD SEAT

(Answering the questions, "Should I accept an invitation to this Board?")

1. Does the company provide director indemnification?

2. Does it have D&O insurance? Is the policy consistent with the company size and maturity as an organization?

3. How do I relate to the CEO—"my kind of person?" Do we have good chemistry?

4. Do I "buy in" to the company's vision? Do I understand its strategic plan? Do I have any serious reservations about where it is heading?

5. Can I determine the value systems of the CEO and his or her current board members? Are they similar? Are they compatible with my own?

6. How is my chemistry with the other board members I have met? Have I had a chance to meet them all? Do their responses to similar questions reveal a deep rift or division on the board?

7. What is the financial health of the company? Does it have a reasonable success scenario on the horizon? Do I understand its current challenges and problems?

8. Does the board have an audit committee? A compensation committee? What other formal committees are currently standing?

9. What is the company's litigations record? Does it currently have any significant outstanding lawsuits pending? Do they worry me?

10. Have I reviewed the financial statements? Recent annual and quarterly reports? Proxy statement and any SEC filings?

11. Have I personally referenced the CEO and some or all of the current board?

12. Is the remuneration for service on the board acceptable to me?

13. Is the calendar for board meetings reconcilable with my current commitments, both professionally and personally?

14. Can I spend the amount of time that will be required to be a virtual 100% contributor? Without reservation?

15. Have I made the case (verbally) for joining this board to a trusted friend or mentor? How did they react?

16. Have I done the same with my spouse? What is his or her reaction?

17. What do I bring to this board? DO I have the experience and skill to really make a difference here?

18. What is my *real motivation* for wanting to join this board? Is it prestige, money, the opportunity to add value, to make a difference, or?

19. Am I excited about joining this board?

20. *What is my gut telling me to do?*

(Reprinted, with permission of Gary E. Liebl, Founding Chairman of QLogic Corporations and the Forum of Corporate Directors.)

INDEX

ABOUT THE AUTHORS

Dorothy K. Light, an attorney, retired from The Prudential Insurance Company as a Corporate Vice President and Corporate Secretary to a twenty-four member board of directors. In addition, she served as Chair of the Prudential Foundation and was the executive in charge of social investments. She was a director of a publicly-held diversified energy holding company, serving as chair of the audit, nominations and compensation committees. She has also served as chair of numerous non-profit organizations. A motivational speaker and consultant, Ms. Light currently lives near Denver, Colorado.

Katie Pushor works as an executive coach and corporate director, with an expertise in marketing and the distribution of information technology-related products and services. Currently, she chairs the compensation committee of a Fortune 500 company, and serves on the boards of a national blood products organization, a medical testing lab, and a community bank. Her coaching practice, Inner Capital, is based in Arizona where she has lived and worked for thirty years. Contact her at **www.innercapitalaz.com** or send a message via LinkedIn.